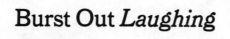

Burst Out *Laughing*

Burst Out
Laughing

Barry Stevens

Celestial Arts
Berkeley, California

Celestial Arts
P.O. Box 7327
Berkeley, CA 94707

First Printing, 1985

Cover design by Ken Scott
Interior design by Paul Quin/QR Inc.
Typography by HMS Typography, Inc.

Made in the United States of America

Library of Congress Catalog Number: 84-045365

ISBN: 0-89087-410-7

1 2 3 4 5 — 88 87 86 85

Barry, who's 82, is relax-
ing to be with. Sometimes we
sit on her balcony in the sun.
Talk might come, or perhaps
not. We might sit for an hour.
I think she looks great in
her sun hat, its shade slic-
ing off over her face and
white hair. With Barry I've
learned that I talk much,
and say very little. Mostly
coined phrases. So I've
pruned my words somewhat.
It helps.

Tarmo Hannula

The world was made for fools.
  Their reckless laughter leaps the facts
  And acts
  Ere passion cools.

  Were but the wise as brave!
  Their ponderous judgments wait for speech
  Till each
  Is in his grave.

  Then call the fools the wise.
  They're better fitted to the earth
  With mirth
  Than wisdom's sighs.

                              Warren McCulloch

At the time *Person to Person* was published, I thought you had to have something extraordinary to become a guru. I discovered that all it took was a willingness to have some people shove you up on a pedestal while they sat at your feet. One man drove from New York to New Mexico expecting to find me surrounded by disciples whom he would soon be one of. I was caught off base. I took him seriously and tried to correct his misconceptions. A good laugh at both of us would have been more apt.

When *Don't Push the River* was published, I was smugly confident that *this* time I had got smarter. Instead of removing my mistakes, I left them in! That would show the guru-makers that I wasn't the right material.

It didn't work. I should have remembered the story told by A. A. Brill in *Abnormal Psychology,* which I read when I was twelve, and laughed hilariously. A young psychiatrist, new to the mental hospital, was sure (like me) he could cure a patient whose delusion was that he was a corpse.

"Corpses don't bleed, do they?" the young doctor asked the patient.

The patient said no.

"So if I prick you and you bleed, you are not a corpse?"

The patient agreed. But when the psychiatrist pricked him, the patient looked at the blood oozing out of his finger and exclaimed, "Gee, whiz! Corpses do bleed, don't they?"

I was fifty years old before I realized that this is *normal* psychology. The only thing that is different is that most of us don't begin with a belief that we are a corpse.

From Eric Berne:

For some people there is something which transcends all classifications of behavior, and that is awareness, something which rises above the programming of the past, and that is spontaneity, and something that is more revealing than games, and that is intimacy.

Fritz: Without awareness you are just middle-class.
Krishnamurti: Without awareness you are bourgeois.
Barry: Without awareness I am trapped.

"There you go again," said a reader of this manuscript, "including yourself with gurus—and then you wonder why some people think of you as a guru."

That is misunderstanding all the way around.

In the first place, people could just as well reject me as a guru. Why not? Most people do.

In the second place, I know that Fritz did not claim guruship for himself, and Krishnamurti says "Don't accept what the speaker (himself) is saying; the speaker has no authority whatsoever, he is not a teacher, he is not a guru, because if he is a teacher then you are the follower, and if you are the follower you destroy yourself as well as the teacher."

I have resisted efforts all my life to make me a teacher and have regretted it when I fell into the trap.

In the third place I have put Krishnamurti, Fritz and me together to show that good thoughts are good no matter where they come from.

And in the fourth place, although I have bracketed our names together, Fritz and Krishnamurti use almost the same words while I say something else—not really different, but that's the way that *I* feel about it. Putting me in a whirl of

BARRY FRITZ KRISHNAMURTI

seems to clarify the whole thing. I'd quote the devil or the president or my neighbor if they made sense to me.

There's miles of distance between teaching and networking. Networking is part of the New Age approach to learning, without an authority who tells us what to think or do. I'm for it.

When I was society editor of the *Arizona Daily Star* in 1922, I replaced Bernice, who had got married. In May it got hot in Tucson—hotter and hotter—and no air conditioning then. I slept in a bathing suit on a canvas cot in the garden, getting up every hour or so to turn the hose on myself and then going back to bed.

One evening as I walked past Frank Scully's house I saw him, with baggage, getting into a friend's Ford. "I'm going to Prescott," he said. A town a mile high and cooler. "Want to come along?" I certainly did, but what about my job? Bernice! I called her and asked "Are you tired of staying at home? Would you like your job back?"

"As a matter of fact, I am and I would."

"Then go in tomorrow and take over. I'm going to Prescott." I hung up and joined Frank and his friends in the car.

I can't do this same thing now, obviously. I never could—the circumstances are always different—but I can make use of the same principle. What is it but awareness and acting in accord with circumstances?

And nobody hurt by that. Not even bumped.

A comic strip from my childhood was called Alphonse and Gaston. They were two gentlemen who were inordinately polite. In one strip they arrived at a door at the same moment and each took off his hat and bowed to the other, insisting that the other go first. Behind them more and more people piled up wanting to go through the door. Alphonse and Gaston were too involved in politeness to notice how they were blocking others and themselves.

For a while I was going out with a man who chased fire engines. No matter where we were headed in his car, on what avenue of New York, at the sound of a fire siren he turned off course and zeroed in behind it and we went to a fire instead. At first this was interesting and entertaining, even a little exciting, but after the third or fourth chase I grew tired of it. At about the same time, he invited me to dinner with his parents, whom I hadn't met. The dining room was large and the space between any two of us at the table would have easily accommodated two more people.

There was a turkey for dinner. It slipped around on the platter when Father tried to carve it. I moved my chair closer to the turkey and took hold of a leg to steady it.

Father looked grateful.

Mother, who had looked disapprovingly at Father as the turkey skidded around the platter, now raised her eyebrows and lowered the corners of her mouth as she looked at me.

Somehow that sums up what this book is about.

At the motel
  i ask, how busy are we tomorrow?
  do you want the day off? they ask
  no, i say, just how busy?
  you can have the day off, they offer
  i don't want the day off, i say
  is it going to be a tough day?
  we can handle it, they say
  but i need the money, i say
  look! they say, take the day off
  okay, i say
  they say, tomorrow's busy but we
  can handle it.

Tarmo Hannula

Focus is a tunnel through which I look at things. Like other tunnels it is a good place not to get stuck.

The breaking up of illusions.
How often I have heard those words, always with the implication that after the breaking up there will be nothing left.
I see myself reflected in a mirror. I smash the mirror.
Is nothing left?

It takes a lot of time to be a genius, you have to sit around so much doing nothing, really doing nothing.
Gertrude Stein

Recognize the wisdom of not allowing yourself to be upset by the eternal confusion, chanciness and tragic-comic nature of life—Donald J. Dalessio, M.D.

Thank you, Donald Dalessio, for reminding me of the chanciness of life. I get so full of my—and other people's—intentions that I forget about that. I'll get around to the confusion, later.

Chanciness begins with which sperm and ovum get together. Come to think of it, the chanciness goes back farther than that. When Bismarck introduced universal military conscription in Germany, one of my grand-fathers—then twenty—left Germany and went to Paris, which he didn't like very well. So after a couple of years he went to London where he met my grandmother who had just recently gone there from Ireland.

Still chancy and a whole bunch of years later, this springoff met a First Mate on the steamer from New York to New Orleans. We got together in wonderful friendliness. I gave him a copy of *Peter Whiffle* to read. He returned it with a poem to me written on the flyleaf, which would have been all right but the book belonged to someone else. It had a limited edition binding.

When I arrived in Tucson, I told Frank, the only person I knew in Arizona, about it. Frank had a friend at Knopf, the publisher, who could get it for me. Chance again.

Right after he got me the book, the man at Knopf wasn't there anymore. He had opened his own offices in the Knickerbocker Building, which was nothing in my life at the time.

After a year in Arizona, which I left because I had fallen in love with a guy who was going somewhere else and numerous other chance happenings and wanderings along the West Coast (I have just remembered two more) I was back in New York because of another chance, or maybe it was several.

...I am beginning to feel them coming down like rain...

And one day I found myself looking at the Knickerbocker Building and was suffused with warm recollections of the man from Knopf who had got me the book. I went in to thank him.

I waited for half an hour, then thought "This is silly!" and got up to go, when the man I had come to see came out of his office with the man who was leaving. It was that close.

I wound up working for him and having great sport with him in Central Park and other places. Through him, I met the father of my daughter at a dress rehearsal of the circus. My daughter was born dying. One doctor came to see her for two or three weeks and then didn't come. Another doctor stopped coming even sooner. I had paid their bills, I hadn't been rude or difficult. Why didn't they come?

I met a girl I had known in childhood (chance again) and she told me that the first doctor had told her family that he stopped coming to see my baby because "It wasn't any use. She was going to die anyway."

That was on Long Island. I thought I would have better luck in New York. One of the people I saw in New York in my quest for a doctor was my old (he wasn't very) boss in the Knickerbocker Building. He had a friend who was enthusiastic about the pediatrician who took care of his little girl when she had a lung abscess.

And so I wound up in the office of a pediatrician who told me that he didn't know if he could help my baby to survive, but he would do everything he could. Honesty and helpfulness. I loved that man although I didn't really see him until ten months later when my baby had been leaping around and acting like a baby for several months. I had a daughter who lived, and nine years later I married her pediatrician and we had a son. Nothing remarkable in that, but now I see ten thousand chances along the way.

But if you want to learn about chanciness, forget all that and look into your own life.

The book you are reading is not the one I thought I was writing but don't let that bother you. It happens all the time. With second order reality lurking in the wings nothing else is possible. We meet at some points, diverge at others, and what you get out of it is rarely what I put into it. And that's all right!

I took dictation from a man in his room at Greenwich Village Inn and typed in another room. The room he spent most of his life in was painted Prussian blue—ceiling, floor, walls, cabinets, bed, chair—everything.

He was writing a book about women. He said in it that women don't use more toilet paper than men, they just rustle it to make it sound like more. The only place where he felt safe, he told me, was on a train. The sound of the wheels on the tracks said to him "Goddam sons-of-bitches, goddam sons-of-bitches, you can't get me now!"

I was used to editing as I typed. Two sentences simply didn't belong there and I left them out. When he read that page he pointed to where the two sentences had been and said "There's something missing here." I said that I had left them out because they didn't belong there. He said "I know they don't belong there but *they've got to be there*." After that I put in every word he said and one day he looked up at me from his bed and said with tears spilling over his lower eyelids, "You're the only person I've *ever* been able to trust."

At the time I knew him he was forty years old, severely hunchbacked, and he knew he wouldn't be likely to live much longer. He had read the statistics. I went to work on my birthday and found him dead in bed. When I got back to my apartment on East Tenth a messenger boy came with a bunch of flowers and I said "Oh no, *I'm* not dead."

Paul Watzlawick in *How Real Is Real?* writes of his inability to avoid the use of words like *reality* and *actually,* which seems to contradict the main thesis of his book: that there is no absolute reality, only subjective and often contradictory conceptions of reality. He refers to the fact that frequently there is confusion between two very different aspects of what we call reality: The first has to do with the purely physical, objectively discernible properties of things and is intimately linked with accurate sensory perception. He uses *first-order reality* for those aspects which are accessible to perceptual consensus.

"It can be objectively verified if I jump in the water to save a drowning person. (First-order reality.) But there is no objective evidence as to whether I do it out of charity, the need to appear heroic, or because I know that the drowning man is a millionaire. On these questions, there are only subjective attributions of meaning. It is a delusion to believe that there is a 'real' second-order reality and that 'sane' people are more aware of it than 'madmen'."

When I was about twenty I went in search of a reasonable man. I knew that *I* wasn't very reasonable and thought that if I found someone who was, some of it would rub off on me. I had a good deal of confidence in the rubbing-off process. I went scampering around up and down the ladder seeking the man at all levels until I was about thirty, at which time I gave up hope and hunting and turned my mind to something else.

One of the places that I looked—the last one—was medicine. There were other reasons why I changed course at this time but that was one of them. I had been doing literary research and always when I finished one job there was another waiting. But then something happened and there weren't any more.

The year was 1929.

At the medical center where I worked next—that has much too sane a ring to it. I spent four days in the employment office of the YWCA before they sent me out to apply for a job that had been filled before I began my waiting. I went back to the employment office and blew up. She went scurrying through her card file and I went to see Dr. X, who was recently hired to reorganize a teaching hospital and a medical college into a medical center. That was his specialty. The work would deal entirely with medicine and architecture. I knew utterly little about either. I tried very hard to give the right answers to Dr. X's questions because I liked him. Two years later I told him "You don't know how hard I was trying to give the right answers." He said "You don't know how hard I was trying to think of the right questions to ask!"

I got the job but it was working for somebody else, which was just as well because I was only going to stay for five months, I thought. I knew I had been useful. It was spring and the medical college had received fifteen hundred applications for sixty-five places. None of them had been processed—evaluated, references written to, etc.— because the woman before me had left in turmoil which had evidently been going on for some time. I knew very little of college transcripts—in fact, I didn't even know what they looked like—but I caught on fast and cleaned up the mess. The confusion, I might say.

Then I told Dr. X I was quitting because I wanted to spend two months of summer with my family—my daughter who was at school in England was coming home, and my companion. "There isn't any chance of your holding the job open for me until the fall?" I asked. "No," he said, "but how would you like to come back and work for me?" "I'll want to go away next summer, too," I told him. "We'll go into that when the time comes," he said. And that's how I had a cush job with a paid two-month vacation all through the Depression. Chancy.

My boss, Dr. X, was a Quaker and came off pretty well on my reasonableness scale, although not 100 percent. The director of the clinic was known as "the highest-paid errand boy in the world." He was paid $10,000 a year in 1932, when $10,000 was a whale of a lot of money. My salary was $1800. The clinic director really did spend all his time doing errands and the clinic ran without him except for this. I spoke to my boss about it and he said, looking up over his glasses, an expression of concern on his chubby face, "Why Miss Fox, if we fired him, he wouldn't be able to *get* another job!"

The dean of the medical college was about forty. He was strong and lean and rich and spent all his spare time mountain-climbing in places like Tibet. One day he went to the professor of pathology to see if he would give up fifteen minutes of one of his classes once a week to make room for something else in the curriculum. He didn't anticipate any difficulty. The professor, a considerably older man, got mad and took off his jacket and offered to fight him over the fifteen minutes!

Three babies died in the hospital at the medical center, having been given the wrong intravenous injection. When my husband (to be) heard about it and remembered the five adults who had died of bichloride of mercury given intravenously by mistake in the hospital where he ran the pediatric service, he instituted the custom of putting a spoon with each bottle. Before giving an injection the nurse or intern would taste it: glucose was sweet, saline was salty, and bichloride of mercury would taste so terrible it would be spat out before it could do any harm, he said. I told this to my boss, the director of the medical center, and he thought it was an excellent idea.

There was much distress about the three babies who died. The heads of departments met every day to figure a way to prevent such a thing from happening again. All but two of the heads were pretty swell guys—not only in my opinion.

After the first meeting, my boss told me the idea of putting a spoon beside each bottle had been rejected by the committee: It was unscientific.

After about two weeks of daily meetings, they met three times a week. Then once a week for several weeks. Then twice a month. I began to think it was a permanent committee. I typed the minutes of all the meetings and was more and more bewildered. They seemed to be getting farther and farther from a solution. They even seemed to forget the problem.

The final meeting was held when they arrived at a solution to the problem of solutions. I read the minutes and my confidence in me was shaken. They *must* be saying something else. I typed the minutes to see if they came out better that way. I went out and walked around the blocks of the medical center to get some fresh air in my lungs and better vision in my eyes. They still said the same thing. I still didn't believe them.

I took the pages, originals and my copies, to the dean's secretary. We often reported the craziness that we saw to each other and sometimes to higher-ups—where we were not encouraged by the results, so that we tended to report only to each other. She read both copies and assured me that I had typed them correctly and they said what I thought they said: hereafter, the solutions that had been in brown bottles would be put in blue bottles, and vice versa.

Too many experts.

Not enough inperts.

I don't have to go to high places to observe nonsense, just look and listen wherever I am.

At the Association of Humanistic Psychologists conference in Estes Park about eight years ago, there was a long table for registration and four people behind it to do the registering. Four long lines of people extended to the other side of the room, where there was an equivalent long table with nobody at it. Then something changed. There were four people at the second long table. A man at the first table made an announcement, pointing to the second table. He said if some of the people moved there they would be taken care of more quickly. Nobody moved. One young woman exclaimed "Imagine! At the *AHP*, telling *us* what to do!"

Although I've got a good deal clearer, there must still be some hangover effect from all the years of living with confusion. When I read what Dalessio wrote of the confusion of life, I felt relief. Somebody knows besides me! I spent a good deal of my life in confusion about the confusion that nobody else seemed to notice.

Confusion began for me—at least that is the earliest I can recall—when I was playing with blocks or something on the floor. I was old enough to keep track of what my mother and her sister were saying, which is younger than we think. A repetitive theme was my uncle Bob. He would die young because of the way he was living and he should save money for his old age. Why on earth, I pondered, should he save money for his old age when he was going to die young?

Occasionally there is a perfect family. Everyone recognizes them and so they recognize themselves. One such family included husband, wife, two sons and a daughter. Then one of the sons suicided. The perfect father told me that his son was in a coma for a month and the father spent most of his days with him, holding his hand. "It was the first time that I saw my son as a separate person," he said, "separate from myself." Of his wife he said "I thought that I loved her. But we were like *this*," he locked his two index fingers together, "and that is not love."

His wife told me, regretfully, that she had done things for—and to—the son "not for him, but so that I would be thought a good mother."

What *is* love? It is impossible to say. I can only say what it isn't. It is not the opposite of hate. Love isn't in opposition to anything. What we usually call *love* (we get smeared with this all the time—as in "I love you, I love you, I love you, you are the ideal of my dreams" and "You belong to me") is part of the world that isn't, the fantasy world we mostly live in.

The world of what is, that's the one I want. It seems to me that we all do but we've got the whole thing so mixed up that we seek in one world what can only be found in the other. It's confusing. It's particularly confusing when I begin to realize that neither of these worlds is outside me.

The Jains in India have a word that means "to the best of my knowledge at this time." *Syat.* They toss it into conversation frequently to remind others and themselves that that is all that anyone has to go on.

I don't know how to pronounce it but I know what it means.

In order to have a good idea you have to have lots of ideas.
Linus Pauling

This book was not written to be read from the beginning to the end which is the beginning, though of course if you want to read it that way, go ahead. "Do anything you want as long as it doesn't hurt someone" was said to me often when I was a child—or else it was said once and repeated itself many times in my head. That meant don't sock someone just because you'd like to. It didn't include imaginary hurts like not inviting someone to go swimming with you when you'd rather go alone.

It was all right to roll a twenty-foot pear tree down the street and plant it in the garden no matter how many people in the village said it wouldn't grow. It did. It had pears. And in spring and summer we hung a big electric light bulb in it, before outdoor lighting had become usual, and worked in the garden until ten or eleven o'clock at night while chatting with the neighbors who hung on our fence of locust posts that had sprouted into a hedge. It was all right for Aunt Alice to buy land near the beach and on the day she "showed" it to prospective buyers it was under water. One of the people remarked that "Mrs. B will be glad to dive for a lot for any customer" and she laughed as heartily as anyone.

Some things worked, some things didn't, and the over-all effect was lively, was living, and somehow or other came out all right at the end. Like me.

It's as if there are two of every I. One of us does just fine whenever he has a chance, but he doesn't often have a chance because he's all wrapped up in a cloak of other people's rules plus some of his own making. That's one of everybody's mistakes. Like playing games for which rules are essential because otherwise how could you know who won?

But if you're interested in getting beyond games, rules get in the way. *Win* and *lose* are words that simply don't apply to living.

Am I the only person who has had difficulties with "acceptance?" I doubt it.

Acceptance does not mean that I have to accept it for myself.

Years ago, Van Dusen sent me a copy of something that had written itself through him after taking LSD. It was beautiful. But it wasn't written in a style that I choose for myself. I couldn't see the beauty of it because I rejected it *for me*. I wasted a good part of several days coming to terms with it—except that they weren't wasted because of what I got out of it. *Then* I could let it be *his*. *Then* I could see the beauty in it.

Acceptance of others' ideas *for them* leaves both of us free.

Clinical experience teaches us that sudden exposure to information of overwhelming magnitude has one of two effects: The victim either closes his mind to the new reality and behaves as if it did not exist, or he takes leave of reality altogether.

This latter is the essence of madness. Yet a very strong argument can be made for either strategy, and this throws us back into a reality "where everything is true and so is its contrary."

Paul Watzlawick

This throws light on the behavior of our neighbor who went to Honolulu to shop as usual the morning after Pearl Harbor, against the instructions of the military. He always went to town on Monday.

But there is another alternative that doesn't come within the clinical experience. That Sunday morning when my body shuddered with vibrations from the bombs, when burning planes were drifting in the bay, and the hangar too was burning—all of which was clearly visible from my home—there were two halves of my mind functioning apparently in opposition, yet they were readying me to receive what I already knew. One part denied, against all the evidence, saying "It *can't* be war"— cushioning the shock—while the other accepted what it knew to be true and sought out what I might do for survival: "If I turned the refrigerator to the coldest setting the milk would keep longer, wouldn't it?"

The expert's clinical experience sheds light on what I didn't understand, but he can't study the people like me who don't land in the clinic. We don't get studied. We're not included in statistics.

There are two kinds of memory. Practical memory is useful. I couldn't even wash the dishes or walk to town without it. I intend to keep it.

Looking at clouds without memory they are purely interesting and beautiful no matter what their shape or color, but I'd better be tentative about stepping into them from a plane.

Psychological memory tangles me in the web of fairy tales of wicked mothers and pure princes and endings which are forever after. They conflict with other people's endings, some of them the very people I have chosen to have my forever-after with. Then I wonder what went wrong between us.

I am better off without it. It doesn't matter whether I accept the Zen statement that speaks of the sin (missing the mark) of permanence or I observe that everything changes. Same thing.

Or is it?

Zen also remarks that borrowed plumage never grows.

When my father was in his seventies he moved to a place in New Jersey that had two roads to town. I visited him when he was eighty. He didn't want to get in a rut. If he went to town on road one all the time, he told me, that would be a rut. If he went on road two all the time, that would be a rut. If he went on road one two times and on road two one time, that would be a rut. No matter what he figured out, it would be another rut. There was no escaping them. He scratched his old white head several times a day, thinking there must be a way out. He died without finding it.

He was in a rut.

The same rut that I was in when I puzzled over which was right: "Look before you leap" or "He who hesitates is lost."

One idea that has been coming into my head repeatedly for years, I have only just now dared to mention: In spontaneity is the only accuracy. A completely spontaneous person would have a really wonderful time.

But I mustn't say that. It's too extreme. Visions of the whole world—when I looked at it with my wrong mind—going beserk, people bumping into each other, getting mad, fighting each other, acting without sense, scared me out of it. But that isn't spontaneous: It's what we have all the time with wars and atom bombs and having trouble with the neighbors.

I knew as a child and have got in touch again now: It is important for people to do what they want to do and not what somebody else wants them to do when this is not in accord with them. It's only about a year ago that I again broke through to my own knowing of this. My ex-son and I had got into difficulties in which I seemed always to be in the wrong. I promised to do what he wanted and did for awhile until I forgot. I made the same mistake over and over during a period of two years strewn with broken promises. Out of desperation I wrote him at last, "You do what you want to do and I'll do what I want to do."

There hasn't been a fracas since.

I used to shudder at making such a statement. Letting people do what they want to do? Suppose their dearest desire is to murder me?

But it's through being frustrated that people even *want* to murder. I know. I've wanted to. More often this has been disguised by different costumes—like wishing that someone would die or go somewhere else.

When I used to have a second thought of letting people do what they want to do, I was in my wrong thinking entirely: Who on earth would want to kill anyone if he were free to do as he wanted? It's through frustration that such wishes arise. It's the conflict between what I want and what I *should* want that produces violence. Then I don't do what I want to do but feel compelled to do what I don't want to do.

When I was successful in suppressing the flow of me, I was approved. But it took only one slip, one unguarded moment to undo the whole thing, and then I was disapproved by my son, and my self was chagrined. I thought myself weak, but it was only my personality which was weak. What was truly an expression of myself—call it integrity, honesty, what you will—had come to the fore.

When I released myself from doing what I didn't want to do, I also released my son. Peace. Harmony.

My trouble was that I was trying to be a "good mother" and do as he wished me to do. But whatever I'm trying to be I'm not. Otherwise, why would I have to try? It was not in accord with me. Then what springs from me runs into what I impose on myself. The two rush headlong into each other. Cross currents within me meet in turmoil. Smash. Crash.

How did I lose sight of this importance? A rule fouled me up, getting between me and my own observations: I must try at all costs to keep relations between myself and my son harmonious. I became devastatingly unharmonious.

A windfall of my saying "You do what you want to do and I'll do what I want to do" is that now when I think my son has been remiss or that he shouldn't have written me what he did or that he hasn't responded to me or hasn't answered my question or hasn't acknowledged something I sent him or any other objection I may have, I am instantly reminded that he's doing what he wants to do and I automatically stop thinking about it. That I've given my permission may be a factor in this.

This is different from being a "good mother" and trying to make myself stop thinking about it, which is putting the lid on, and a lid that has been put on can blow off. Whereas this no-thinking is effortless. I feel as though my mind is cleared of a whole flock of entanglements.

Whee. I feel free and present.

It is easier to say what spontaneity is not than what it is. It is not even a vestige of rules. It is what operates in an emergency and "There is no time to think." It is observation-understanding-action without an intervening period of thought.

It is un-training: disconnecting the brain from psychological memory, so that nothing interferes with right action.

Right action is seen moment to moment as things happen, the person always in accord with the happening. *I* is not present—no interference from thoughts of I. No self-interest.

So what is?

The sparkling moment, the being in freedom without thought. Nothing binding. There is neither acting nor reacting. Just is.

The ball hits the racquet hits the ball. The person meets the person with the freshness of no-remembering, and the sky and clouds and earth are simply part of all, together is all.

I sob as I write that, remembering.

No I.

I had worked in a medical center for five years. My husband was a doctor. I had a whole bunch of medical taboos on the tip of my tongue. One of them was *never* take medicine that has been prescribed for someone else. I have just realized that this is another rule—or was.

It gave me the creeps when at the ranch in Arizona someone felt rotten and described his symptoms and someone else would casually toss him a prescription bottle saying "Try this. It helped me when I had something like that." I needn't have shuddered. They were tentative in their trying and didn't have any strong drugs around. If it was unhelpful, it was discarded before it did any harm. This works out better than taking something because the doctor prescribed it when all my senses are shouting NO!

There were many things at this ranch that are not approved by hygienists. One glass beside the kitchen sink for thirty-five or so people. Manure tracked in on the kitchen floor. There were twenty children and sometimes they had a manure fight in the corral where the older children were milking. It tended to get in the milk. There were maggots in the meat-cutting table. But when I looked around at the *people* they were unusually healthy, rarely sick, and not plagued by all the little ailments that beset people in other places.

Health must have some interchangeable parts.

I am not and never have been an expert. There is no reason for you to accept anything I say as true because maybe it isn't. You're on your own. Same as I am.

And same as the experts are, only usually they don't know it.

I remember when the experts came in fashion in the twenties. It was then that we first heard that we mustn't try to teach our children. "You might make mistakes!" Leave it to the experts. For a while, that included not teaching them to brush their teeth. Don't take care of your children when they are sick. Get a doctor! The experts told us it was wasteful to have a parlor and not use it except on occasion, and what had been available as a meditation room got lost as we flung open the doors to the living room.

All the experts assured us that if *we* did things we would make mistakes. So we made theirs instead.

Remember: The joy is very important.

Brahmananda

I read that forty years ago and it was my first real introduction to Vedanta. I decided it was worth studying. More recently comes Norman Cousins, who used laughter along with medical treatment to get out of sickness and all the others who say that laughing is good. Why do we need to be told, when it *feels* good?

More than any other time in history, mankind faces a crossroads. One path leads to despair and utter hopelessness. The other to total extinction. Let us pray we have the wisdom to choose correctly.

Woody Allen

When Steve decided to publish 3000 copies of *Person to Person,* he did most of the work. We both went around gathering information. I went to Bob Yamada of the Berkeley Book Co-op to find out how much discount book dealers get. He said we'd be apt to lose money because the book wouldn't sell.

I expressed confidence in the book and in word-of-mouth. He said "Oh it isn't that, but when people who've heard of it go to the bookstore and ask for it, they look it up in *Books in Print* and it isn't there, and they don't know where to get it."

I reported to Steve. A few days later he was getting information from the vice president of Stacey's in San Francisco and he mentioned this.

"Oh, I should think you could get a listing," said the man.

Steve wrote to *Books in Print,* which was about to go to press, and he got three listings for fifteen dollars.

Sometimes the wind blows in the right direction. It does seem to favor those who are lollopping along on their own.

Nothing real can be threatened

Nothing unreal exists.

I read that on the first page of *A Course in Miracles* and it hit me with such a whammo (which means I knew it already) I wrote it down in my address book. I didn't want it to get away from me. I needn't have worried. I don't think I've ever referred to it.

The rest of the book did not appeal to me. I used to think that I *should* read the whole book but now I know better—in fact, as well as I did before that. Everything appears in myriad forms and another will reach me easily, and that's *for me*. On the other hand, maybe at some future time the *Course in Miracles* will be more meaningful to me. I cannot rule out the possibility.

There seems to be good and bad everything, and "trying" is one—no exception. There is the kind of trying that really is lying. I'm trying to love you in spite of—trying to overcome what is, and not accomplishing it because it can't be done that way.

The other kind of trying holds the meaning to sift, to cull, to sort out. There's nothing wrong with that one that I can see.

I once had a book that didn't make sense to me at the time I had it and did about fifteen years later, when it was out of print. I advertised for a copy in *Saturday Review*. I got a few answers from dealers in secondhand books, as expected. What I didn't expect was all the people who wrapped up a copy and mailed it to me. I was at the Quarter Circle V Bar Ranch at the time, where the mail came twice a week in an enormous mail sack designed for a maximum load for sixty-five people. Each mail was heavy with copies of the book. We had to have one of the ranch hands hoist it up above the refectory table and dump them out. I gave copies to everyone who was interested in having one and then began on the libraries. Redistribution of surplus wealth—and what fun.

It would have been awful if it hadn't ended.

Physics will go on forever making better and better models of the universe and none of them will ever be the universe.

Jean-Paul Vigier

We put what are only ideas into little boxes and then forget that it is we who put them there. When someone takes them out and looks them over—maybe redistributes them—we scream as though a law of the universe had been violated instead of upheld.

Like the rules of marriage (who should fix dinner, who take care of the children, when and whether the wife or husband may go out with anyone else and if so, with whom), our notions of capitalism and communism—for that matter any beliefs which we have.

"Never take no for an answer"—what a mistake that often is. In Arizona in 1923 I thought I wanted a loan from the bank to buy a horse, to save him from being sold for use as a polo pony and (fate worse than death to me at the time) shipped East.

The bank turned me down.

Two months later I was in San Francisco. What on earth would I have done with a horse?

In 1925 I asked my mother to lend me $25 a month so I could rent an apartment that I liked. I forget what street in New York it was on but it was a nice apartment—everything furnished and in good shape and surrounded by other apartments lived in by people who were also furnished and in good shape. My mother said No. I wound up in a basement in Greenwich Village with a kitchen stove in the bedroom, which also had a fireplace and water taps in the bathtub which was enclosed by a thin wall. It also had a door. When you opened the door you stepped into the tub. I wrote while the two young walk-ons who lived upstairs took my two-year-old daughter for outings in Washington Square and papered the bathroom walls with rejection slips. The house was mostly occupied by young people, which I also liked, and living there was a romp.

Often I have been steered to somewhere I wanted to be by having someone say no.

This has happened so often that when I hear no I look around hopefully.

"Be careful what you set your heart upon for someday it shall be yours." And when I unset my heart upon something I breathe more deeply and feel more free. Narrow escape.

Have we been attempting to impose rules for countless centuries under the illusion that by trying to enforce them we are in control?

I was working in the red-rock country of Arizona with a construction crew of about two dozen Hopi Indians and a Hopi cook. One day as I entered the cookhouse I saw Mona Lee, the cook, talking with a new Hopi worker. As I came in, he stopped talking. Mona Lee, whose back was toward me, gave a nod of her head in my direction and said "She's all right."

Mona Lee, her three children and I and my two did not eat with the Hopi men. We waited until they were through. The evening before when we were at the table, her older boy spilled milk on the plain board table. I said "Oops, Chile, lap it up" and pushed his head down toward the table. With a gleam in his eye Chile lapped up the milk, and Mona Lee said "You are not like other white women. They say you must get the mop. By the time you get the mop, the milk is on the floor."

By "other white women" she meant of course those she had come in contact with—mostly teachers in the Indian service. I teach you.

Instead of teaching rules, why not share our observations and that way we'd both come out ahead—without indebtedness and recriminations on either side.

When Devi Prasad was at the Gandhi Training School in India, a thirteen-year-old boy asked him how to go about writing a book. "I don't know," said Devi, "but I should think that someone interested in writing a book would know how to go about it."

Five boys each spent ten hours a day writing books until they were completed. They also illustrated them. The school was very poor and had only black ink, and for brushes the boys took the hairs from cows' ears and bound them together. They also bound the books.

On their own.

My sister, her husband and I were all three of us quite young—twenty to twenty-six—when we got into a triangle. One evening in the kitchen the triangle became a tangle and my sister and I threw ourselves into each other's arms. We had, as Tarthang Tulku would say, "emotionals." Then we burst out laughing. We had at the same moment seen ourselves as characters in one of the melodramas that we thought funny. Then we became aware of her husband standing outside the enchanted circle and looking as though he—who was supposed to be the central character—had been left out. We laughed again—and again when we each made a move toward him that was intended to comfort him. We saw ourselves from inside and outside both at once. Our joy was unconfined and we felt wonderfully healthy. Recommended for inclusion in holistic health.

After Pearl Harbor, I considered the possibilities as I saw them and I thought that I would be a Gray Lady. I went to the nearest hospital and tried to present my own unique talent. I could write letters home for the men in hospital who could not write because of illness or injury and in their own language, so that at home they would know that the letter was indeed from them and not from some intermediary. But the woman who interviewed me was not interested in my talent. She talked of uniforms and dress uniforms and whom I would take instructions from and hours.

We lived in the country and hadn't enough gas for an extra trip to town. When I had to go to Honolulu early in the morning with my husband to see the dentist or to do something else I spent the rest of the day like this: I walked along a street of stores (I have only now seen myself as a street-walker) and sometimes in less than half a block, sometimes a block and a half—no more—I was picked up by a soldier, a sailor, or marine with a most urgent request. What did I think he should buy for his girl who was majoring in art but had switched to physics? When he had chosen something, he bought me an ice cream soda. We parted—both happy. In less than half a block, sometimes a block and a half, I was picked up by a sailor, a marine, a soldier with a most urgent request. What did I think he should get for his mother who . . . As we walked, we talked and a picture came through to both of us of what she might like to have. The purchase made, we had sodas and said thank yous and goodbyes and I went walking down the street until . . .

I didn't tell anyone. That kept it perfect. It wasn't my idea. It wasn't planned. It just happened. I loved it very much. It helped to sustain me through all the difficulties with my husband, exacerbated by the war, and his difficulties with me, and all my mistakes in trying to figure things out. As I was asking the wrong questions of course I didn't find anything worthwhile.

Although my difficulties with my husband went on and on, my shopping trips with the military ended. I don't know how. No matter. They were absolutely perfect and they still are. No yesterday and no tomorrow.

We're all different to begin with and so is what happens to us. Even when the sending is the same to two or more of us, our receivers are different. Glenn noticed this when he went to a movie with three friends and afterwards they talked about it. They had seen four different movies. A French film director observed the same thing when he said that a movie doesn't happen on the screen; it happens between the screen and each person in the audience.

When two people exclaim "Isn't a fireplace wonderful!" they may think they are in agreement until they start to build a fireplace. One person's fantasy was of a small marble fireplace with a mirror over the mantel and accoutrements to match, while the other had in mind a rough stone fireplace with hooks to hang pots on and the smell of hearth bread.

My childhood recognition of differences came about through observing the differences between my sister and myself. At dinner, if we misused or mispronounced a word our father said "Get the dictionary!" I enjoyed doing this and was fascinated by the dictionary. My sister hated doing it and hated dictionaries. This and similar observations led me to remark "You just can't cook all geese at the same temperature."

About thirty years ago I became interested in memories. I wrote my sister mentioning things that had happened, to see what her response would be. In each case, her reaction was different from mine. A boyfriend of hers who had made a great impression on me, she had forgotten. The bathtub on the front porch had embarrassed her, which surprised me. At no point did we remember the same thing in the same way.

Interchangeables

How far is it in miles or time?
  How much is it in time or money?
  What do I lose in money or life?

Paul was going to come at about nine o'clock this morning. At 9:15 he phoned to say that he had forgotten he had a class. Would it be all right if he came around two o'clock? Certainly. It made no difference.

Everything in me was fine until about three-thirty that afternoon when he hadn't come. I began thinking about it. Right away I was cross. It seemed somehow that he had done me in by not coming—although every single statement that I made to me to that effect turned out to be 100 percent fallacious:

He was being very inconsiderate. Just how he managed to do this, I couldn't find out.

He was wasting my time. My time hadn't been wasted. I had gone on doing what I had to do.

He was holding me up on getting my work done. See preceding paragraph.

And so on. On and on.

At this point, I was not doing my work. I was just angrily thinking about how I couldn't do it.

Who was doing me in?

Why is it that when someone steps out of line there's a rush to get him back in, instead of an interest in where he is going?

Nothing is completely itself unless it is whole and then it is indescribable.

That thought came into my mind full-blown. I knew what it meant. Say anything about a person, a thing, an idea, and it is an abstraction. Taking a piece out of the whole. It can never be everything. Words can't do that.

When I was sick, I thought if the doctor held a bunch of layers of me up to the window and looked through all of them at once, he might understand me better, come closer to the truth of me—closer to all of me.

When I try to put everything I know (or think I do) in my head at once, I blank out. Then I am closer to knowing.

All the rest is partial. Some of it is useful in helping me to get around in this crazy mess of confusion but that is its only value. Most of it is junk.

Gestalt: the whole is greater than the sum of its parts.

When my daughter was nine she made a joke about the ants that got chilled in the butter in the ice box. She referred to it—over and over—as the anti-freeze mixture. When I told her that I thought that once was enough, she said, "Well, it's my joke. I can use it as often as I want."

I'm sure that I wrote about what follows in *Person to Person,* which is the same as saying it a hundred-and-ten thousand times. But dear God! I remember it so vividly now—the pouring of water from a bottle into the little glasses we used for painting in school. My utter joy in seeing the flowing water, the accuracy of it, flowing in an arc from bottle to glass, the sun making colors in the water—all this happening at once was magic.

Then the teacher said when I had gone all around the class with this magic "You did that *very* well," and the glory departed. In its place I had chestiness. The teacher had praised me. I was back in the "real" world.

This seems to be the same thing that Paul Watzlawick describes:

"If oil is poured from one vessel into another, it flows in an arc of utter smoothness and silence. To the beholder (obviously he is speaking of the mature beholder) there is something fascinating in the glasslike, motionless appearance of this rapid flow. Perhaps it reminds us of that aspect of time whose mysteries are even greater than those of the future and of the past—the infinitely short present, wedged in between these two infinitely long expanses extending in opposite directions. It is both our most immediate and our most intangible experience of reality. *Now* has no length, yet it is the only point in time at which what happens, happens and what changes, changes. It is past before we can even become aware of it and yet, since every present moment is immediately followed by a new present moment, *Now* is our only direct experience of reality—hence the Zen Buddhistic simile of the oil stream."

When I was a child, it felt more like an orgasm.

"There are many things that can be predicted very accurately—for instance, planetary motions, the tides of the oceans, chemical and physical events, the fact that if I don't step on my brakes I shall run over that pedestrian, etc. But notice that awareness of these aspects of our first-order reality does little to relieve the general uncertainty of life.

"It requires a very high degree of maturity and tolerance for others to live with relative truth, with questions for which there are no answers, with the knowledge that one knows nothing and with the uncertainties produced by paradox."

It is only another way of looking at Time. There is no difference between Time and any of the three dimensions of Space except that our consciousness moves along with it.

H.G. Wells

41

When I was twenty and announced that I was going from New York to Arizona, my father was very angry—so angry that I slept for a couple of nights on the fire escape. I thought he had gone mad. I was only doing a very minor version of what he had done in leaving London for Chile and jumping ship at Tierra del Fuego when he was twenty. Why was he so upset?

Fifty years later, I found out. He had been instilled with the idea—whether by himself or someone else I don't know—that he was responsible for his daughters until they were twenty-one. How could he be responsible for me when I was in Arizona where he couldn't keep track of me?

My painting/drinking uncle's family name was von Raacke but when they came to America his father thought they should have a good American name so he listened in New York and chose the name of Bergman.

Bob—my uncle—started out working in a blacksmith shop in Manhattan where my mother's sister found him, married him, and sent him to art school, where he became one of the directors. He had his own theatrical scene-painting studio that did 85 percent of the theatre scenery in New York in the twenties, some of which got in Encyclopedia Britannica. When he was well into his seventies and I expressed my longing to return to Arizona, he told me "But you can't live on scenery."

Steve was twelve when he first met my uncle. He came home from school one day and Bob was there. Soon he was showing Bob some Indian artifacts from the Southwest. Bob took a stone maul in his hand and studied it. There was a piece missing from one end, which made it look sort of like a crown. His face lighted up. "King Charles!" he exclaimed.

Steve studied the maul to see what Bob had seen in it and his face had just begun to register comprehension when with a twist of his wrist Bob changed the scene. "Raisin bread!" he said.

Bob was sitting at a table in my father's living room. Behind him was a painting of Great Salt Lake after sunset that had been in our family ever since he painted it when I was a child. Now he said with a backwards nod over his shoulder "Get soap and water. Clean it."

I was dubious of my abilities but I got Ivory soap and water and a sponge and began lightly washing it. Flecks of paint appeared on the sponge and there were equivalent white spots on the painting where the canvas showed through. "The paint's coming off," I told him.

"Let me see."

I held it up.

"Ah! Mist on the marsh. Beautiful. Scrub some more!"

When they were both nearly eighty, my father talked about the earlier kings of England and their debauchery.

Bob listened, a beatific expression on his face. When my father stopped talking, Bob took the cigar out of his mouth and said softly "It must have been *wonderful* to be a king in those days!"

My father looked baffled.

At another time my father talked about Mayor O'Dwyer of New York commendingly. Bob listened. He was really very good at listening. He said "Yes, yes," agreeingly all the way through. When my father had finished, Bob said, "But ah! Jimmy Walker! Best mayor we ever had. Went out *every* night."

My father was a North of England peasant, a Wesleyan, with all the rules of honesty (as well as other rules) tucked securely under his belt. I heard him say once to my uncle "What about the radio those girls stole from you? Did you get it back?"

"Yes," said my uncle Bob comfortably. "Got another one just like it. I got it back."

"What about the thousand dollars Russell Janney owed you? He must have made a great deal of money on *Miracle of the Bells*."

"Oh, he did," said Bob and cheerfully almost merrily he recited how many hundreds of thousands of dollars Janney had received from each of the foreign rights.

"What about your money?" my father persisted. If the debt also persisted, it was at least forty years old.

"He still owes it to me," said Bob, sounding happy with the rightness of his world and everything in it.

When I was in my fifties, I was sick and broke and suffering greatly from not being able to do anything about either one. My ego was hurting, bunched in a knot in my chest. Added to my miseries, a man lent me $400 and wrote me that I was not to mention it to him, that he hated to have people say anything about it, while at the same time he implied that he couldn't afford to lend it to me. I tried to make that into a clear statement, which was impossible. Money, money, money. My head ached with trying to figure it out while the rest of me went on agonizing over my inability to take care of myself.

I had a dream of some brightly dressed riders on horses galloping along the Great Wall of China. One of them stopped and picked up a gold piece, then tossed it away again as he rode on.

Money just wasn't that important, wasn't worth keeping myself sick worrying about.

I recognized the rider who stopped to pick up a gold coin and then tossed it away.

He was my uncle Bob.

The gold-diggers of the twenties were after him, of course. He would take them out to dinner and that was all. Two girls said immediately after dinner "You don't mind if we leave, do you?" and Bob said easily "No. I don't care how soon you go."

Frequently, the girls tried to get him to write a check to them. Just once, he got so drunk that he complied. He got so very drunk the bank wouldn't honor his signature.

One evening after dinner with uncle Bob we were walking back to his studio. When we came to Times Square, he walked across to the middle going against the traffic. It looked like the parting of the waves as the cars went around him. When he got to the middle I saw him stop beside the cop who was directing traffic. I saw the very tall cop lean down to lend an ear to my very small uncle. Then he blew his whistle and before I could step off the curb he came to me, swept me up in his arms, and carried me back to where my uncle stood waiting. There, he put me down and my uncle and I resumed our walk to his studio on 39th Street.

As we walked, I asked him "What did you say to the cop?"

Bob took the cigar out of his mouth and said "My niece. Go get her."

Bob never gave Christmas presents to anyone. That was his rule, it seemed. But one Christmas when all the family were together, he stood in front of the fireplace with a bunch of papers in his hand, and fanned them out so that everyone could see that they were the mortgages he had on their houses. Then he chucked them into the fire. Nothing was said by anyone. There was a lovely feeling in the room.

My aunt worked as a secretary to Judge Learned Hand and as a court reporter—daytime hours. The nature of Bob's work—theater—kept him up late. Often he got home at three in the morning. They sometimes didn't see each other for six months. Looking in a store window with a friend my aunt said "Don't look now, but there goes my husband."

So it was at the family gatherings—Thanksgiving, Christmas—that my aunt had a chance to tackle him about things that had been smoldering for some time—like the Depression. It was the Thanksgiving after the Crash at a family dinner that she could ask him how his stocks were going. "Oh fine, fine," said Bob tapping the ash from his cigar. "Broker called me up just yesterday and asked for another thousand dollars." My aunt and his sister (who was also my aunt, as she had married one of my mother's brothers) exchanged glances and when the party broke up they zeroed in on Bob. They had similar notions of what a husband should do and be and ganged up on either side of him, practically pinning him against the wall as they battered him with criticism of his behavior—regarding stocks and other expenditures. He didn't resist.

He didn't do anything. I don't know what went on in him but I suspect the answer is nothing. When they were so thoroughly involved with themselves that they didn't notice, he just walked away. But I doubt that he knew this. He simply had built-in perfect timing.

Resisting without resisting. My painting/drinking uncle had the knack of that. I never quite got the hang of it myself.

Last night I was sleepless and thought again of Bob. I wasn't trying to remember and I wasn't trying not to remember. Remembrance just came. I forgot about going to sleep. For three hours, each time I thought that I was done with recollections something else came to mind and I laughed again.

Each time when remembrance faded I thought I must surely have ended the stories about uncle Bob. Then another one appeared. At last there were no more stories and I went to sleep. But just now another one has surfaced.

Ruth Draper was the monologuist of the twenties. It was a habit of hers, off stage as well as on. She had been performing engagingly for some time in Bob's studio and I think that all of us had had enough. Dessert is most enjoyed in small quantities. Bob gently took her arm and elbowed her to the stairs—two narrow, dark flights of them—from his studio to the street. Ruth walked down them backwards slowly as she continued her monologue. Bob stood at the top watching her descent and waving his hand in farewell, saying over and over "Yes, yes, lovely, goodbye, yes, yes, lovely, goodbye, yes, yes, lovely, goodbye," pleasantly but firmly and with emphasis on goodbye, until she went out into the street.

As he went back into the studio, Bob looked pleased with his accomplishment.

That is *my* uncle Bob. My sister's uncle Bob was different.

The mind, not being an object, no two perceptions are alike.

The Buddhist Bible

Resisting without resisting.
Doing absolutely nothing.
Not reacting.
No perception.

My parents were atheists but I didn't know that until I was about thirteen. They let us go freely to any churches in the village. We both started out with the Baptists who had a hole in the floor for dunking but then we branched out. My sister went to the Dutch Reformed because she liked their theatricals while I went to the Episcopal because they gave nicer Christmas presents. I went to the Catholic church a few times with my best friend but I didn't like that. It was too exclusive. She was permitted to do in the church all sorts of things that to me were forbidden—like doing something with the holy water.

I learned more about "churches" in this way than I possibly could have if my parents had told me about them, and in a much more flexible way. I couldn't have passed a quiz on any of it, but to this day that knowledge is right *here* available to me at any time. *Words* cannot possibly reproduce this learning although I can select some to write about it. What I have written is a small part of the whole.

Gestalt: The whole is greater than the sum of its parts.

When I was writing *Person to Person,* Carl Rogers remarked on the fact that my writing "about" the various articles took as much space as the original articles I was writing about. I knew that it was necessary for what I wanted to do but I didn't latch onto the *how* of it.

But if you will take something that you have experienced—no matter what—and explore what you picked up about it without effort and contrast this with what you learned from a book, you will see the difference.

I learned more about differences and sameness in churches by going to a lot of different ones than I could have from books or people. It's a different kind of knowing.

I read a book about the Hopis that was said to be good and I thought so too. Later, I began working with Hopis. Still later, I read the book again and put it down saying "Where are my friends?" I couldn't find any of them in the book.

Words have to be said one at a time, saying one thought at a time, and even the order is pre-determined. There's nothing wrong with words but there is a lot wrong with the way we use them. In the apprentice system, words are used *in connection* with the action. The *whole* is taken in. Gestalt again.

It's much more interesting than school where so much of the *action* is left out.

I wrote a letter to Paul asking him if he would like to plerk (play/work) with me on writing a new book of etiquette. He did not respond. He came to see me several times after that and did not mention it. This was all right with me. Then he referred to my letter one day, beginning with an apology.

"That's all right," I told him. "Everyone should feel free to ask anyone anything and everyone should feel free not to answer."

He was visibly and audibly relieved as he almost sighed his yes.

Apologies are either real or fictitious. In either case, what's the point of making them?

When I was working for the Prescott (Arizona) *Journal-Miner,* one of my jobs was to get news from the sheriff's office. One day he said "You can put it in the paper that we've got a motorcycle cop on the Black Canyon Road now."

"I didn't know that," I said.

"Oh we don't have one," he said easily, "but if you put it in the paper, it will make people slow down some."

Doing the best you can with what you've got. The old American way.

A person can suffer any kind of punishment, may even be shot to death for violation of a *code*. What someone *believes*. Isn't that ridiculous? Obviously some people don't think so. Or perhaps they live so much within the code that they can't see it.

People mostly object to my not accepting something as a gift when I don't want it. They think all sorts of things. That I don't like it and 'it' becomes *them*. It may just not fit with my life at present. Why should I have to accept it and keep it if I don't like it, have it take up space, require attention and protection? And so on and on and on.

On the other hand, my rejection is sometimes spurious, based upon what someone else whom I admire didn't like. I admire you and you don't like X so I don't like X. Second cousins twice removed.

Why am I considered rude if I say I don't want it and not rude for the other person to foist it on me?

Suzuki said that both he and Hu Shiu were murderers of the Buddha—as I am in writing all this—but that it is not a bad thing to slaughter him if it does some good for somebody. This writing is good for *me*.

A thing for me to watch out for is when my skull feels like concrete. A thing for me to be aware of is what I *don't* know. My skull then feels aerated. A door has been opened, letting in the breeze of not knowing.

Try it, if you haven't already—for no other reason than that I like company.

How happy I am in the breeze of my not knowing! On this gray and cheerless day I am gurgling like a brook or a baby.

Does anything real happen with intention—or is that all part of the theatrical scene, the make-believe, with which we have surrounded ourselves?

I don't remember how many years ago I read that Krishnamurti said all escapes are the same, whether drinking, drugs or religion or anything else. This made some kind of sense to me although I was far from clear—sort of looking through a glass darkly.

Yesterday I went to town and stopped at the gem shop. One of the young men there had just recently been overwhelmed by a young man from India who lived according to numerology. My friend was greatly impressed by the thoroughness with which he had absorbed it and showed me a book which the young man had given him. I looked at it in a scanning way and told him that I had given up on numerology in my twenties when at a large party of people who were strangers to me I "did" numerology. I told a woman that she was an obstacle to her husband. Many people later, I told a man he had contempt for all obstacles. Still later I learned that they were husband and wife.

I quoted Lucretius to my young friend—*nec Babylonios temptaris numeros*—or, don't be led astray by the Babylonian numbers. That came from more than fifty years ago.

Do whatever you like with that one—as with everything else.

Next morning I awakened with a clear understanding of Krishnamurti's words—*my* understanding. All escapes begin with *concepts*.

When I begin with a concept, this comes from my head.

It is secondary experience coming in first. I think it's something real instead of just a tool. If I knew it was just a tool, I wouldn't take it so seriously. Not worth fighting over, certainly. Who, over the age of six, would fight over a hammer? When *real* comes first, the whole scene changes.

I usually—perhaps always—like the person beneath the cloak of concepts.

It seems to me that my mind did a skid there from drinking, drugs or religion to concepts. And yet, with what I now see/understand about people and concepts, I am totally satisfied. At peace with the world, at peace with myself.

"Make haste slowly," my born-and-raised-in-Ireland grandmother used to say.

"When I hurry it takes longer," as Jim Klee and I observed.

And still I am amazed that what works in the short run, like doing the dishes or walking to school, works also in the long run, like writing a book. I know that I shouldn't be surprised, but I *am*. Everything's made up of moments and the only difference between short and long is more moments.

When I am in the place-that-isn't-a-place I can easily know it. Everything in my world is right and will be forever in that place-that-isn't no matter how I louse up otherwise or afterward. If I give you every cent I have when I am in the place-that-isn't, it is still all right tomorrow, even if tomorrow I wouldn't give you a paper clip.

I bought two bottles of Sage's ginseng and then it seemed best not to take it any more, so I gave it to Paul, who uses it in his practice. He wanted to pay me. "Take it," I told him, "and then my mistake will have been corrected." As soon as I said it, I knew it was true.

So much better than a trip to the store to return it and all the bother to the storekeeper—and what a joyous moment.

When I was twelve, my best friend and her older sister used to talk about how a girl should be with a boy. I listened, then went home and practiced in front of a mirror until I was sure I had it perfect. Then I went out and in the street there was a boy and I just talked to him. When he was gone I realized what I had not done and was chagrined. I was a terrible failure. I just couldn't remember what I should do.

I was thirty-five before I learned the rules of society (through my husband, who had known them practically from infancy) and then I felt clever.

I thought for a time that I had got the hang of life, but in fact I had it by the throat, choked until there were only a few gasps left.

I had learned enough of the rules imposed by the social order—the twentieth-century American social order—for this to constrict or stifle me. But I felt sure of myself and my knowing and attributed my feeling stifled to something else, or else wondered where on earth it had come from.

Now I breathe again. Really breathe—not, as one man described my breathing in the past, "It's like a whisper."

I remember when I decided to give up all remaining pretenses. I didn't know what the first one would be. That evening I was invited to have dinner in a French restaurant. My host left the dessert up to me. I pointed to the menu and asked the waiter "What's this?"

My host looked mortified. I felt happily honest.

Sixteen-year-old Marlene put on the dress she had just bought and asked her mother "Do you like it?"

"No," said her mother gently—she never spoke any other way.

"Wahoo," wailed Marlene with tears.

"I only said I didn't like it—I didn't say it was a law," said her mother with extraordinary good sense.

Marlene stopped her ranting as though she'd got her perspectacles back on.

To stay young
I have to watch
all the time
to see that the old lies
don't creep up on me
and convince me.

When I make a rule of something I don't realize what I am saying: That one way is okay, all other ways are not.

Rigid.

It doesn't really matter if it's how to use a knife and fork or blow your nose or how often to take a bath, or things one doesn't do in public or words one doesn't use, or what to eat with your fingers or who it is permissible to go to bed with—anything that makes you think "I would never do that" and feel a bit superior.

I accumulate these year by year and become sad for my growing old. I used to have more fun. I mis-attribute my growing old to my added years.

Right at the moment I make—or accept—a rule I become prejudiced. Anyone who doesn't live by my rule is a little off, at least. Then, if I am well-intentioned, I struggle to accept the other, make excuses for him—after all, he isn't enlightened—try to be nice to him, show that I am a tolerant person.

The person I shouldn't tolerate is myself!

Not condemn. That's the same trap whether I condemn myself or another. Wholeheartedly break my own rule with awareness and see what happens inside me.

It's so easy to live! And so hard getting the hang of what's easy.

What four straight lines made without lifting the pen from the paper connect all the dots?

No rules equals anarchy. Everyone knows that.
In awareness there is no anarchy.
No dis-order.
No need for rules.

When I was a child I thought my heritage was galloping over the plains or jouncing along in a covered wagon. My parents arrived in this country only a few years before I did.

I like *heretic* better than heritage which is mostly fiction anyway.

Heritage is not *now*.

A heretic is one who holds controversial opinions in any area. What opinions aren't controversial? Who isn't a heretic? Particularly if he goes to the next state or country or moves into another subculture.

In New York in 1934, my husband was a "pale pink." When we got to Hawaii a month later, he was a "red." He really hadn't changed that much on the way there. In fact, his opinions on Russia hadn't changed at all. His environment had changed.

Patriotism is one of our earlier mistakes that looked like a good idea at the time. Now we can see how its unity is divisive. It is also like languages—it means something different according to where you are — Poland, Italy, Cambodia . . . Confusion. It has the sound of glory in it— but really it's just competition.

People can be patriotic about a town too. I heard a man on a bus say proudly to his very small granddaughter "You're a New Yorker!" Weren't there once wars between cities? Then countries. Then it went global.

I do hope no one believes what I write. It's so much better to find out for yourself.

Now I know that Swami Vivekanda really meant it when he said "I shall be sorry if you believe what I say."

A confident man is a dead human being.
J. Krishnamurti and B. Stevens

A man in a psychiatric hospital watched himself on TV and said with surprise and dismay "I want to be gentle and kind and I sound like I'm wearing army boots."

A discrepancy he might have been aware of without television.

When my sister had had enough of triangularity she asked me to leave her and her husband—entirely friendly.

She was very much a friendly person. I was not so amiable. A flood of angry words rushed in behind my forehead. I loved my sister too much to say them. I cut them off, nipped them in the bud, and stopped them like a traffic cop who will not let them enter. Immediately I saw the whole thing clearly, untainted by second-order reality—another name for fantasy—all of the nonsense washed out. A week later I was on my way.

This happened to me at some other times—as when a member of the faculty plagued the academic vice president and president—once he got them up at two in the morning—for ten days telling them that I was a Communist. When the matter was finally brought to my attention, all ten days of it, I felt overwhelmed by all the faculty gossip that had been going on. It was such a mess that it couldn't be put straight. I gave up. At the moment I gave up, the whole picture came into my head as if I were seeing every leaf on a tree. Total understanding. I said "Forget all that. Just tell him I still love him."

Immediately I had said it, I thought "That won't be acceptable!" But it was. Everything calmed down.

I always thought of these instances as something that came to my rescue when I was really in a fix. It never occurred to me—as it does now—that this was something I could cultivate like any other talent.

I have thought too often that I did not know enough to say anything, which of course is true but neither does anyone else and if we all come out in the open we may find ourselves with a whole new world to live in—just by unmaking the old one.

Everybody's in the same boat—some forward, some aft, some midship. If I want to see both ends and the middle at once, I have to get out of the boat.

Americans, said Tibetan lama Tarthang Tulku, have too many choices.

Like checks, cars, hairstyles, trousers, candlesticks, books, magazines, professions, jackets, tools, catalogues, furniture, dresses, dishes, shampoos, computers, movies, games, dolls, stereos, vacations, planes, soaps, kitchen appliances, towels, nostrums, water purifiers, fixtures of any kind, collectibles, and everything else including Do-you-want-Cheddar-or-Swiss-with-your-omelet? and What-shall-we-have-for-supper?

Take closets. When I was too broke to afford a room, I thought it would be so nice if someone would let me use a closet to put my things in while I wandered. I didn't find an empty closet anywhere. I found closets packed full though—lots of them. Too much. Their owners had difficulty choosing what to wear out of so many. I thought this strange. *I* wouldn't have any difficulty.

But when I became more prosperous and had more clothes—still not nearly as many as those of my friends—I found that I had trouble deciding too! I started giving things away. When someone accepted something that I gave them from my closet, I felt grateful to them. When they had gone I opened the closet door just to enjoy the space that was left.

The more I give away, the easier it is to choose what I will wear.

Scarcity is nice. Not deprivation. I don't know anyone who likes that. I learned about scarcity at Navajo Mountain, where many things are scarce and mail came only once a week. Letters were read in an entirely different way in the silence of the mountain with so much waiting in between.

What don't we have in too much variety? (I can think of a few but none of them are things.)

Takes too much life and time.

It doesn't do any good for me to have found the perfect item that I could be content with having year after year because next time I need it, it isn't there or they've put something new in it—"new and improved"—and I must start looking all over again.

Only one way out that I can see. Choiceless awareness seems to be the only choice.

Better that than going to bed with my head full of choices and trying to decide which one.

Choiceless awareness.

How do I arrive at it? I am asked.

When I am aware, there is only one way to go at this moment and no other moment exists.

I once saw/heard through an open window a tall, broad and very embedded-in-politeness man say to his very small son, in a pleasant-sounding undemanding tone of voice, "Would you like to get the newspaper from the mailbox (at the gate) for me?"

"No," said his son, answering the question matter-of-factly, not in the least rudely.

The father blew up, with all the bigness of him. The son reacted with a tantrum, which the father did not understand.

By being polite, the father expected to get what he wanted. His command was so deeply embedded that he couldn't find it himself. "But I only *asked* him," he said when I tried to explain what I had seen happen. He had accepted a code so thoroughly that when it didn't work, he first exploded, then tried all the harder with the same code that had failed him in the first place. Even when there wasn't a big boom, there was small explosiveness all the time. It seemed to me he went off like a firecracker constantly and like a cannon sometimes. He was very much like Mt. St. Helens, if you can imagine her controlling herself between blows with politeness.

I was the man's wife. I had vowed when I was young and didn't know any better to make him happy—not knowing this is something one person can't do for another. My husband fostered this by telling me that I made him happy. When he was not happy I tried hard and was so intent on my trying that I couldn't be aware of the one significant fact: I wasn't getting anywhere.

I have seen welfare workers and employees of the Indian Service and teachers and others make essentially the same mistake. When what you're doing doesn't get the results you want you try all the harder making the same mistake. "If at first you don't succeed, try, try, try again" doesn't allow for changing course.

Awareness—or the scientific approach—would have provided a different response. It seems elementary that I would then have checked to see what *results* my efforts were getting, would have noticed my success or failure and—in this instance—would have changed course.

If I had been aware sooner I would have saved all of us years of misery and stress.

I am reminded again that it is all melodrama no matter how I may elevate it to drama.

Maya. The world of delusion.

"You mustn't say that!" is not a good thing for a person of any age to be told. It makes me shut up, at least momentarily, and this shutting up makes me clench my jaws. Then I have to go to classes in relaxation to release them.

I am thought to be a responsible person (by others besides myself) when I can keep a secret, but what it does for me is make me rigid, chopping off spontaneity. It's part of thinking first what I am going to say. The *freedom* to say anything doesn't mean that I'll *say* it. Awareness takes care of that easily. Besides, there may come a time when it works out better for you if I don't keep your secret.

It wasn't exactly a secret that I tumbled into when I was first at Deep Springs and the Weinreichs were over-busy packing. They said they had promised Miss Mastellar, who was going to Yosemite with them, that they would leave on Thursday, but it was really too soon. When I was with Miss Mastellar, she was overly busy packing because the Weinreichs had said they were leaving on Thursday. I had put my foot in it often enough to be wary: Maybe they didn't mean what they said. But when the same thing was going on next day with a little more frenzy because there was less time, I decided to take a chance. I told the Weinreichs what Miss Mastellar had said.

They let out the breath they had been holding in, which is also not good for people—the holding in—and one flopped on the floor and the other on the couch. I then went to see Miss Mastellar. She let out a woosh! and sat down.

Most secrets operate in the same way. If you are not aware of this, watch any soap opera.

*R*omance: *"not based on fact"*

says my dictionary.

"Trash!" said my friend Cora of the soap opera that another friend was watching on TV. Then she burst out laughing because she had just seen herself in a soap opera of her own making—"love," conflict, jealousy, misunderstanding—all the fantasies that were occupying her mind practically all the time. "I wish I could always see it that way," she said, ruefully aware that she wasn't always going to.

The other half of the split cried on my shoulder (figuratively). "Why does it always have to end this way?"

Why does a bubble always burst?

More than twenty years ago I had a difficult time convincing Carl Rogers that it was important to me to be able to write to him freely and that he didn't need to answer my letters. When he writhed (my perception) I writhed. Writhing is kinking, is not the easy flowing from which so much happens.

Once he was convinced, he sounded easy too. He sent me copies of his papers as they came off the ditto machine and wrote me a note when he wanted to and could, usually expressing his disagreement on some point or other.

Eventually all this led to the writing of a book that could never have surfaced if he had not permitted me to do what I wanted to, which was no bother to him once he had got the rule about answering letters out of his head.

He liked it too.

When I first began reading novels it seemed to me that if anyone in the book had made simple uncommon sense, the story could be told in two-and-a-half pages.

Then I got indoctrinated into the lie as Kafka put it, and read novels and suffered with the people in the book. Could anything be sillier? Well, yes. Next, I actually wrote novels.

Now we have movies and TV as well to smear us with folly and take up mind space.

Surd means "lacking sense." Sort of like the German who was learning English by himself and was overheard in his room saying:

I haf a gold mine
Thou hast a gold thine
He hass a gold hiss
She hass a gold hearse.

Or like me when I am afraid that I may mislead you with words when only I can mislead myself with my nose hooked to the carrot.

We have certainly put a lot of steam into making ourselves comfortable from the *out*side. When I go to other countries like Australia and Chile, I recognize old discomforts from my childhood and youth. But somehow we always louse up in terms of overall comfort, or ease. Hence drugs, liquor, groups, and all the rest of the escapes.

How about trying a leap out of the future/past and into the world of what is? I'm not there now, but it sure helps to have been there.

When I was twenty-seven I read a book that spoke beautifully of the evils of jealousy. I was very happy because I had been rebuked for not being jealous when I *should* be. How many shoulds do we pick up in the course of life? I'd hate to list them. It would take too much time.

With great enthusiasm for a man who didn't know jealousy, I met the author of the book. He was a very dear person. I was glad to know him. But of himself and jealousy he said—which was not what he wrote in the book—"I manage to behave very well but I get *awfully* cross inside."

Squabbles between people are always *past* or *future*—sometimes both—no matter how *present* the people may think they are. They are never *now*.

Break a window or smash a car on the telephone post outside it and the spell is broken.

An Angry Young Man working with gestalt grabbed a down pillow and struck furiously at the chair in which his fantasy mother sat. A seam of the pillow broke. Down rushed to the ceiling of the room we were working in and gently floated to the floor, filling most of the room.

He forgot about being angry and laughed.

I is a singular of which the plural is unknown. Erwin Shrodinger said that.

I has a certain validity to it. Well, an uncertain validity which becomes a lot more uncertain when it shifts to *we*. *I* like you. Clear and definite. Of course it may also be a lie. *We* like you. Do we? Or is one just going along with the other for the sake of peace. Well, for the sake of uneasy peace which isn't peaceful.

Let's throw the whole thing out and go for a walk.

Whatever we do is being watched and censored. Actually it is not Big Brother who is watching: It is Big Me.
                                                            Chögyam Trungpa

He said that although his clock which he had just received was very like mine, it was not as good as mine. It made no difference to me, one clock or the other, and I told him we could swap if he liked.

He thought about that—at least that's what I imagined he did with the time that he said nothing—then "No, I'll keep this one, because . . ."

"No *because*," I told him, out of my very recent rediscovery that becauses are meaningless.

"No because!" he said happily.

Tai chi is zen is dhana is meditation is yoga is gestalt is awareness is t'ai chi is zen—and I have to put them all in a circle and start anywhere to know that.

My father was a North of England peasant who went to London to learn a trade. He taught me to do everything without force. "Easy does it" wasn't just words to him. "If you have to force it, then something's wrong. Find out what it is." When I was sixteen, he taught me to drive a car, first briefly telling me the simple mechanics. After that, he sat beside me while I drove saying "Listen to the gears. Listen to the sound of tires on the road. Listen to the engine . . . smell it. Don't expect the road around the bend to be the way you think it is. Don't expect the driver of the car ahead to make sense—maybe he's a lunatic."

Be aware, alert and sensing, living and moving in harmony, with no grinding and no crash.

Awareness springs from nothing out of nowhere.

Everything else starts in my head which is an attic full of junk.

Mother used awareness when making clothes for my sister and me. I realized that as I was going over a lot of things when I was sick (1953-56) and sorting them out. I wondered why it had never bothered me that my mother sewed for my sister vastly more than she did for me. I got the answer when I remembered my mother saying of me "She doesn't care what she wears if she has one good dress in the closet." I knew it was true.

If my mother had been imbued with my father's notions of fairness, I would have had more than I wanted, my sister less than she wanted. We would both have lost out.

When my first child was born I was appalled as I held her in my arms at the power that I held over her. I must be very careful how I used that power.

Somehow that first thought stayed with me through all the evidence of something else. There was also her developing power over me, which I was not aware of. There were all the other influences in her life, which I was only faintly aware of in spasms. There was herself and her own choosings. There was herself and the radio, which said things I did not agree with. When I tried to discuss this with her, I lost to the radio. She was nine years old. Tenaciously she clung to what the radio had said. Whether she was right or wrong is not what I am considering. She and the radio got together and I had no power over her at all.

Yet I still felt responsible for everything she did!

The culture in which I was embedded insisted on it and this got between me and my own observations.

I choose to give up suffering.

This doesn't say the same thing as I choose to be happy.

One is a negative.

The other is a positive. Always be positive! But then I start with a picture in my head of what happiness is and I limit myself before I start.

Whereas when I choose to give up suffering—a strongly positive act, I see now that I have written it—I notice when I am suffering, look into the cause of it in myself, and give up whatever makes me do it, leaving the space wide open to whatever comes in. It isn't easy, but surely is a ladder to heaven.

Of course, I'm also giving up luxury—the luxury of feeling sorry for myself. I am then one step beyond where feeling sorry for myself is possible, seeing the whole thing clearly.

I burst out laughing.

We will temporarily, or if possible permanently, delete from our vocabularies such words as physical, mental, organic, psychological, psychosomatic, and somato-psychic to avoid verbally dissecting the human being into artificial segments.

Wallace Ellerbroek

I wish I knew Ellerbroek, I thought on reading that. It's so much easier to correct something when someone else is making the same corrections and you can correct each other as well. But who says he is? Maybe he just thought it, like that chap who wrote about the evils of jealousy. Anyway, I don't know Ellerbroek and I'm not about to go practically from border to border—Canadian to Mexican—to find out if he really knows what he's writing about or if he's just worked things out intellectually—no connection with the rest of him—so I'd better get busy myself.

It seems to me I don't use any of those words very much except inside my head and inside my head I am using some of them most of the time. Auwe! How do I get at them? It's easier noticing them when I've said them— more like snipping them out of a piece of paper. But in my mind, they slide past like something slippery. Before I can see them properly they're gone, dived to the bottom of the lake before I have a chance to grab them by the tail and yank them out. But I'll have to find a way to do it or stay where I am, and that I can't bear.

I blinked. Like the magical wish in a fairy tale, the genie in the bottle, the answer came to me in a way that I couldn't possibly have thought it because all my thoughts are old. What was going on in my head now wasn't words, though words could come out of it—inaccurately, I realized a moment later. Or was it a second before?

The voice that wasn't a voice but could become one said inside me that I would be wasting my time going about it in the old way. No, it didn't say that. I *saw* that and put words to it, somewhat like putting words to music. What was presented to me was a shortcut. As nearly as I could express it in words—though actually words distorted it—was more like a bunch of pieces that moved around and showed how things went smoothly together. What this told me was that right in the beginning of movies in my head was where I should do something. Like forming a different image of man that would automatically replace the old one. You can't see red while you're looking at blue.

I have a circular mirror made in China. The frame—about two inches wide—is carved except for one place where for several inches it is left untouched. I enjoy that blankness.

The Navajo rug weavers always left an opening at the edge of a design.

Rules are probably all right if you wear them like Oriental and Indian art, which include space for you to sneak out of.

There are two methods of doing anything. There is the one-two-three method and there is the no-method. Originators have used the no-method. Otherwise they couldn't originate. Others have used the one-two-three method under the impression that they were following the originators. This has been going on throughout time. The one-two-three people just can't get the hang of no-method, and bastardize every new idea that comes along. As there are more of the one-two-three people by a long shot and as the others have some degree of one-two-three in them, no-method is constantly losing out.

People aren't born with or by the one-two-three method.

When I put the one-two-three method first I block off the no-method which comes first or not at all.

Montessori used no-method to a high degree in her teaching of children and with unsurprising success. This is apparent in her writing where she described what she *did*. She made observations of the children and checked them out. For instance, she put the materials away in the closet at the end of the day and noticed that the children seemed to want to do this. She asked them. They did. From then on, she let the children put the materials away.

Another word for no-method is awareness. It also has a scientific ring to it.

Interested people to this day who wish to do well by the children and replicate Montessori's success are often using the Method which has been put into a Manual. One-two-three. What has been lively goes dead except for those who use their own no-method more than they do the Manual.

To be able to follow the originator you have to be able to follow yourself and be your own originator.

I have read that our method of education began in the Middle Ages when it was thought that everything was known and that if all this could be packed into the young they would be thoroughly prepared for life. Now we know that what we know is very little and that we need to get more *out of* the young, old, and everyone.

I don't know what the Middle Ages were in the middle of but they were certainly a long time ago. We're trying to extricate ourselves from not just our own past, but from centuries of making the same mistake. The New Age is just beginning!

Suppose instructions were given to an unborn baby:

"Now do this . . . and a little more that . . . whoops, a little less. Next . . ." How could any baby be born naturally if he were being *told* what to do? The instructions could only be partial because of all we don't know about borning a baby. Besides, who could resist saying "Whoa" when it was time for dinner?

My respect for the Dalai Lama increased when I read a long interview with him. His most frequent observation was "I don't know."

Creativity gets bypassed when a picture is "painted" using a design with numbers and a key saying which colors are to be used where. Or powdered soup labels tell me to "Be Creative! Add sliced frankfurters!"

When things are put into my head and I act from there it is never as good as if it comes from what feels like all of me. From my head is too limited and inflexible. Too resistant to rearrangements. This is just a sketch done with crayolas. Or call it groundbreaking. A hole made by a shovel doesn't look much like an excavation.

Once upon a time, people thought they knew or that they should know so they pretended to. Parents, doctors, teachers, psychologists, scientists, philosophers, mathematicians . . . all pretending they knew more than they did. And some poor fools like me went along with them. Fortunately not entirely.

But something is changing. Parents and teachers—some of them—have been discovering that they don't always know best and that the children whom they thought they knew best *for* were remarkably capable of knowing better. Some doctors are now making the same discovery about patients and are giving them information on which to base their own choice of treatment. A psychologist even admitted in court that he couldn't predict behavior. Scientists—one that I know of anyway, so *a* scientist—makes his hypotheses known to the public and invites them to take part in proving or disproving them.

The one scientist that I know of is Rupert Sheldrake, who proposes a new theory of life. When I thought with enthusiasm of his throwing things open to the amateur as well as the professional I thought of myself as a bandwagon hopper. Then I remembered that nearly twenty years ago I had presented in *Person to Person* my own evidence for including both the amateur and the professional. So was I instead one of the precursors?

How can it possibly matter? If others hadn't got the same notion, without them my notion would have died. What does *credit* or *who came first* have to do with *life?* We're all in it together.

I had known Troll since he was fourteen. One of his parents was very conventional. He had been living for some time first with one parent for six months, then the other for six months. Somehow he slipped between them.

When he was twenty he lived for some time in a cave above Palo Alto, meditating at sunrise and sunset, and in between gathering leaves and berries to eat, supplementing them with chapathis which cost him five cents a day. He said that the same diet wasn't nearly enough for him in Palo Alto.

One night he spent at George's when I was also there. He was going to leave next morning, to head north or south. "I'll know when I get to the highway," he said.

We got a postcard a few days later saying that he was going to Mexico. "They'll never let him in!" exclaimed one of his friends. "Nothing but the shirt and pants that he has on, and his long hair, carrying nothing." "Oh you know how it is with Troll," said another. "When he gets to the border, all the guards will be looking the other way."

He sent a postcard from Oaxaca.

When he returned, he mentioned that he had "got awfully yellow" while he was in Mexico, and he was very sick. "I figured my body knew what to do about it better than I did, so I just lay there until I was well." He returned to Palo Alto with rosy cheeks.

He hadn't expected to hang around in Palo Alto but he got busted for pot and fined $500. He got a fairly respectable shirt and pants from somewhere, cut his hair, and went looking for a job, which he found interesting. When he couldn't think of anywhere else to look, he sat under a tree. He found a job, worked until he had paid off the $500, and then he started on his way again.

No harm to anyone.

His eyes sparkled like dew drops in the morning sun.

Chick was milking the cows—seven of them—and I was leaning on the corral fence waiting for the next pail of milk to be carried to the separator. He talked of the cows as he milked. He told me how this one insisted on being in one particular corner of the corral, that one liked to be talked to—wouldn't give her milk without the sound of a voice—the other one liked him to lean against her, while another one didn't seem to care as long as he remained silent.

"Just like people," I said.

"I should say so," he exclaimed. "There's no such thing as a *normal* human being."

I had noticed that myself.

One of the meanings of *normal* is "free from mental disorder." Try and find one! As the Quaker remarked to his wife "Everyone is queer excepting me and thee, and thee art a bit queer."

Life is much easier when I don't except myself.

Labels are for bottles not for people.

My father was a man who Kept His Word even if his word had been given only unto himself. I admired my father. I too Kept My Word. (I might just as well have chosen to do so because my father didn't.)

Slowly I learned to make as few promises as possible and not to take other people's promises too seriously. It's remarkable how I do this all myself!

I am no longer a nobleman whose word is his bond.

This is much easier on all of us. What I used to hold myself to I also held others to. If I kept my word, I would jolly well see to it that they kept theirs and give them hell if they didn't.

It's much easier on all of us to be flexible. "I will if I can."

It fits reality better too.

Think how much forwarder I'd be if I had never looked backward. And what did my looking backward accomplish?

When a flash from the past comes into my mind, that's all right, as long as I don't hang onto it, develop it, let it take over my life. The more I develop it—while thinking that it develops itself—the farther I am from the truth. More fiction in my already fictitious life.

> Don't bother trying to correct what is wrong—just make energetic progress in the good.

> Don't let your toes curl over the past: All your energies are needed in the present.

> I take the energy that goes into pouting and use it to write another song.

All sound advice, whether it comes from a swami or from Duke Ellington.

I was eighteen. That seems so long ago and at the same time no distance at all. A young man had taken me for a drive. There was a bend in the road concealing everything ahead. On our right a heap of crushed rock, much higher than the car. Around the curve came a car on our side of the road, heading straight for us. The road was narrow and on the other side it went down like a cliff.

I went completely still as we tilted at a seemingly impossible angle. My friend had taken the only possible alternative to a smash: He drove on the side of the mound of crushed rock. I leaned toward the mound.

The other car whizzed past. My friend's car was back on the road. He said "If you'd said *anything*, we'd both be dead."

That was another thing that happened at times. I was grateful for it. I never thought of it as something I could cultivate. I didn't believe the magic of it. My body assuming a position that I hadn't thought of, to do what it could to balance the weight. The sound of the wheels as the crushed stone skidded under them. A world sharply defined that encompassed nothing but this and was at the same time as vast as the universe. The stillness that penetrated even the crushed rock. The absence of fear.

Observation/understanding/action
without an intervening period of thought

Like if a baby falls in a swimming pool and you forget
to remember that you don't like babies or don't like
white babies or you don't know how to swim and you
jump in and pluck out the baby without even thinking
I'm being heroic.

If you think about it later you are watching a movie of
your own making and can (and do) change it in any way
you like.

Real is unchanging and unchangeable. You can't do a
thing about it except move on.

There's a paradox there.

What I do with paradoxes beside live with them comes
later.

If I hadn't had so much gobbledygook poured into me by
parents teachers neighbors relatives children (all of
whom had had it poured into them) think with what a
clear mind I could have gone swimming.

Man is not a source of information. He is a sink. Some
scientist said that. When I think of all the pourings into
all of us and out of all of us and into all of us . . .

It makes as much sense as alphabet soup.

It's amazing how uncluttered I can be. Scads of things and
people disappear when I stop thinking about them.

In God we trust. Not likely. But if we did we would have the method of relaxation that supersedes all other methods. It isn't important that we trust in God but that we trust. Then we relax and when we are relaxed we make better sense than we otherwise do.

What keeps us from it?

It seems to me that we don't trust people or events to behave the way we want them to. Funny kind of mistrust.

I either can do something in an emergency or there is nothing I can do. I am much more likely to discover that I *can* do something if I make myself quiet and wait. Sometimes that is the best something I can do.

The present heals. No jet lag.

When I was flying to Chile from Los Angeles—13 hours, with a time difference of five hours including allowance for daylight time—I deliberately did not think about either end of the journey and just enjoyed the clouds, the sky, my body, the travelers, the steward, the stewardess, and sleep. I arrived in good shape. I have had trouble flying from Albuquerque to San Francisco: When I got there I felt as though my front had arrived but my back was still in New Mexico.

All of me arrived in Chile at once and I was very much together.

I've read many times what Chuangtse is said to have said about the futility of argument. Why don't I say it myself?

When I was about thirteen I was frequently amazed when the other children conceded that I had won an argument. I knew that I was wrong yet I had convinced them that I was right. What was *that* all about?

At eighty, when I feel in need of support and think of someone who would agree with me, I realize that this would prove nothing but that he agrees with me.

And the same if I call in someone who doesn't agree with me.

If I call on someone who differs with you and me both, then he will differ with you and me both, and if I call on someone who will agree with us both, he will agree with us both.

Who shall I ask to judge between us?

We end up at the same place we started, so why bother to begin?

If I am intent on getting every word that someone says or writes because I believe he has all the answers or to pass a test, I am tense.

If I am intent on accepting only what I believe to be true and rejecting the rest, I am tense.

Now I have gone back to an earlier mode—listening or reading without questioning.

What? Without questioning, I'll accept what I don't agree with!

When I went to hear Krishnamurti talk in Ojai for three weekends, he spoke from a platform that had been put up among the live oak trees. I sat a little distance off, behind and to his left. He came through quite clearly on the loudspeakers. I was not intent. I was looking out over the fields and trees and sky and I heard him without trying to hear. It was not a question of believing or disbelieving: It was a matter of understanding. When I understood, it became a part of me in a flexible sort of way. Each time I latched onto something strongly. I have not found it necessary or advisable to dump it in the years since then, unlike a lot of what I learned in school.

The only way to test anything is to try it. Try lying back and listening the way you would to what the wild waves—or the pine trees—are saying confident that although what they are saying may not always be true, it still can lead me to the truth, not by believing the words but by observation of what goes on in me.

Tuned too taut, the music flies
Tuned too slack, the music dies
Tune me the sitar neither high nor low

Intellect? It comes in later as secondary experience. We have twisted ourselves around so that intellect the splitter comes first. Then it's difficult to have the primary experience in which we are whole.

The hardest thing is remembering to be aware. Everything else is easy.

                                    Satchidananda

My life seems so easy when there is no hanging on. To what?

At Lake Cowichan, Fritz Perls asked us all a question and waited for answers. This person said that and the other said something.
   I said nothing.
   He said "Barry?"
   "I'm blank," I said.
   He nodded and went on to someone or something else.
   How nice to have my blankness easily accepted.

Another word for blankness is *space.*
   Enjoy it!

When my sister was twenty-four and I was eighteen I went to live with her for a while about twenty miles from Buffalo. She had two small children and a husband.

One evening at dinner we got into a dispute over whether it would be harder for a woman who had been at home with the family to go out and get a job or for a girl who had been working two years (me) to take over a family. We decided that we couldn't decide by talking about it. We'd start off next morning and find out.

At six-thirty next morning my sister went off on a train with her husband to look for a job in Buffalo while I ran up the hill to the farmer's for milk.

My sister came back in the evening after having worked as a laundress in the Hotel Statler all day. It was the only job she could get in a hurry.

What my sister had to contend with, I don't know. Everything I did, at first, the four-year-old would correct me with "My mommy does *this* way." How irritating it was until I said "Pat! I'm *not* your Mommy." She never mentioned it again.

I didn't even know how to diaper a baby and looked to two- month-old Marc for guidance. If he seemed satisfied, I figured I was doing okay.

There is no way to tell you briefly how ragged I was run between getting breakfast for four, getting the milk from the farmer up the hill, splitting myself between the four-year-old and the two-months-old with the four-year-old always at my ankles no matter what I was doing. I had never done anything like *this* before.

My sister admitted defeat on the fifth day when she quit her job. I couldn't rejoice at my victory because I knew I was about to give in. But the curious thing is, we both felt we had proved something for all time when we hadn't proved anything except for *us* at *this* time in *these* circumstances.

Or had we?

This book has been growing—down, not up. That seems a good way to get to heaven.

When I was a child and expressed how things seemed to me, other children shouted "Sez you!" I was bewildered. Of course I said it. Anything that came out of my mouth must be from me.

With time, I "learned" better. With still more years, I unlearned what I had learned.

These are some of my observations about life. Of course, they may be wrong. They may all be wrong and even so may lead someone—by their very wrongness—to something that is right.

Another way of saying it is that I am freed to speaking on my own authority—though what that means is questionable. I just looked it up in Webster and know less than I did when I was confident that I knew. I like knowing less. Think about something you know and check the feeling that comes with it. Think about something you don't know and see what feeling you have.

Then you have proved or disproved what I have written—not for me and not for all people for all time, but for the person you are *now*.

I am speaking for myself.

Always trying to find answers that will last forever when nothing does.

I was eating a cupcake. Some cupcakes I like but this one I didn't. Furthermore, the things that are in it aren't good for me. There was no one around but me.

The cupcake had been baked in one of those fluted paper cups. When I had finished eating the cupcake, I started eating the crumbs from the cup.

Whammo! I wake up and leave the last few crumbs in the paper cup. I have seen rule No. 746 in action: *Eat everything on your plate.* Still operative.

Eighty years old, and I still have the same habit—not a bad one, mind you, except that like all rules it sometimes gets in my way. Like now.

I can't break it, after all these years.

Oh can't I?

Awareness does the trick.

That holding back anger and its various relatives is not good for me—unless I deactivate it—I have known for some time. That holding back *truth* is not good for me is very recent—like a few days ago.

I have kept to myself the notion that the world would be in better shape if all of us acted spontaneously, without an inkling that I was doing myself harm. Yet when I released it—on a page that has so far not been read by anyone but me—I felt so much better than I had. The goodness of it showed in improved typing and in general relaxation, which of course are linked.

Now I see that holding back is a form of holding on— which certainly is obvious but I didn't see it. Another bad thing about holding back is that then I conceal the truth from me. It surfaces in my mind briefly a couple of times a year instead of being part of my everyday functioning.

Some years ago I asked my inner self why it did not show me the truth more often and it said "Well, you always pull down the shades." Here is another example of how I create my own blindness.

I looked over the scene in its entirety to discover whether holding back was *always* bad and saw that the answer was yes. It is the *action* that is bad for me. If I was easy about what I was holding, it wouldn't be holding back.

When I tried to explain the what-when-why of my holding back I got into such a tangle of untruths and half-truths that I could make no sense of it. Second order reality.

Image of myself trying to swim through a mess of branches under water. I made no headway.

Ridiculous!

If I saw someone doing that I'd know they were crazy. Wouldn't you?

I can't promise to do as you wish. Your wish has been noted. What happens depends on future happenings. Your wish may have changed, anyway.

No praise, no blame. You can't have one without the other, and *both* cancels me out.

I sometimes like to do things *to see* what would happen. Test them out. It scares me some that people who work with bombs and related weapons may have the same notion. Just before World War II, we had a visit from a man whom my husband had known since World War I when they were both prisoners in the Schartzwald. The friend had stayed in the army and was sent to Hawaii before Pearl Harbor. He said "Of course I want a war. It's what I've been trained for and I want to see how it works."

That's got a funny edge to it. It's bound to, but I haven't been able to find it. I offer a prize of $25 (provided I have that much at the time) to the person who finds it.

I am the funny edge! I had amnesia for a while.

Now I remember when I was sick in the hospital and seemed to go so far out into space that everything on earth was seen in a different way. One of the things that was different was that I could see my body lying on the bed and realize that if I died it would be very funny to see people come in and treat with respect what was only my *body,* left behind like a cloak that I didn't need any more.

"Nothing real can be threatened . . ."

Have you ever tried to be unbusy? I was surprised to find that it takes as much time as being busy.

There are no bad people. There are only people who see things differently, and react to what they see.

When I first realized that I was an actor fulfilling the roles and scripts and interactions that were assigned to me in some distant past beyond remembering—like everyone else—I was uncomfortable. A world of apparitions. But then I saw all those spooks taking each other, themselves and the world they've made quite seriously, as if it were real. They-we even *call* it the real world! As if they hadn't made it up themselves!

    And I laughed
             and laughed
        and laughed.

We hear more and more all the time how new technology can better keep track of people and what they're doing. It gives me the creeps. Pretty soon they'll be able to keep track of what we're thinking. What defense will we have?

I imagined us going around carefully thinking nothing so that we couldn't be tuned in on.

Then I burst out laughing.

I had remembered when I was sick and Steve came home from college at Christmas. He came in the door with two friends and almost immediately said something that referred to his father—in my mind, not necessarily in his—and I became afraid that he would pick up what was going on in my mind. I most carefully did not think—no fantasies at all. For days I focused on things around me in the apartment, on Steve, on people walking in the street.

I picked up a little desert glass bottle and said "Would you like to take this back with you?"

He said "What's going on? Ever since I've been back, as soon as I think of something you give it to me."

When I first wake up in the morning I stretch. Then I laugh. At first the laughter is artificial but soon it becomes ridiculous and then it becomes real laughter. I learned that from a yogi.

Much better than laughing at jokes which I don't think are funny. Why don't I do it more often? I'm not living alone. A rule gets in my way. What's yours?

Permission. Why do I always need permission?

As a child, I said that it seemed silly to cry for someone when they died because it seemed to me that if the tears were real, I was crying for myself. I was rebuked for being callous. I have just now remembered how often that happened. I didn't *feel* callous but eventually the grown-ups wore me down and made me sentimental. Now sentimentality gets in my way and I need permission to get out of it. Please! Won't someone give me permission not to be sentimental?

Big Me censoring *me* out of existence again.

Orville went over this manuscript, marking each page plus or minus. He marked most of them plus. Then he died. I meant to write to him and I hadn't. I felt bad. Sentimental. What on earth difference did it make to Orville if he had heard from me or not? Anyway, he had enjoyed the manuscript before he died.

I was on the beam again.

Or was I?

I remembered

> *Kinsmen's sticky tears clog the departed.*
> *Let them go easily, cheerful, whole-hearted.*
> *The Panchatantra*

With that, I smiled and went *happily* through the rest of the day.

Hi, Orville!

After one of his lectures a woman told Swami Vivekananda "I understand what you are saying—that life is a school."

Vivekananda snorted. "A school? It's a circus!"

When I find something or someone—a piece of cake or a person—irresistible, I don't choose to resist.

It was wonderfully dark. Susan, Karen and Heide talked around the fire. The children played with fire. I lay on the sand a little way off. Mostly I just heard and smelled the river as it rushed over and around the rocks. Just paying attention. I know the importance of doing that. I far from always do it.

Last night beside the river I did, and after a while from inside me came something that wasn't words but that changed and became the words "All the mistakes in the world don't matter." All the historical mistakes as well as those going on now.

Like everything else, this can be misused. The original statement comes from my interior. My intellect can take it over and do almost anything with it and that is a sin: It misses the mark. What came with the feeling and then with the words was ease, and with ease I am much less likely to make mistakes. There's nothing to make a mistake about.

I wrote that five or six years ago. I knew it was right and lacked confidence in my own observation. Now, Gene Gendlin uses the same knowing in his therapy and I have confidence. Will I ever get over needing confirmation? Ridiculous!

A tranquil atmosphere makes for fewer mistakes.

Hal Linden

I don't like being possessed. Do you? It can seem awfully nice for a while. To be wanted. To be needed. To be attractive to someone so they want to keep you. But, according to your tolerance, it wears off fast or slow.

Children are possessions, although it is apt to be the grown-ups who see children in this way. To the law, they are possessions.

Not to me.

The prison is your family.
You work in the yard helping the lemon trees.
One limb has surpassed the fence and
one night you go.
Having memorized the pattern of thorns
you zigzag up and over.
You rent a jeep, using a globe for a map.
It feels good.
There are leaves flapping in your hair
whistling along the open night.
One hand caresses the globe, the other, the wheel.
You see some people on the shoulder up ahead.
You speed past them.
It's your family, smiling in the darkness
eating from a basket of lemons.
You love them.

Tarmo Hannula

When my under-age son took off in his Model A without telling me where he was going and when I woke up at one or two in the morning and he wasn't home, I trusted him, and if there was any trouble I was sure it was capable of explanation . . . but oh, I expected there would be trouble with the neighbors because I didn't know where he was. Visions of myself as Bad Mother haunted me.

Torture by the ghosts of things that never happened!

Reflections of reflections of reflections of

Through kitchen window ivy-covered wall with reflection of sea seen through livingroom window and silhouetted pair of legs wrong-end-up feet waving in many times reflected air. Ivy leaves come through ocean waving greenly. Sun fiery setting on mauve horizon in window of nextdoor house and to right is setting with surf and seagulls. Stereo in backwindow ivy is on buffet in livingroom in muted colors.

Wall of glass livingroom and beach is, surf is, horizon is, sky is, and all is reflected in side window reflected in front window where human shadows dance or are they reflections of shadows?

Nextdoor room is here fuchsia tree with purple/red blossoms outside window candle burning indoors burns brightly outdoors in leaves of tree.

Kitchen window ivy reflects ceiling light in diningroom and front window sky is dotted with bright lights reflection of lights in livingroom and this does not necessarily say anything about time of day may be degree of fogginess or forgetfulness or state of mind that needs light to brighten world outside that got dim inside and became intolerable when taken back in.

Mirror. Two mirrors. In them glimpse fuchsia tree, indoor garden, god's eye, mimosa tree, an already dippy Klee becomes more so.

And sometimes all this mixed-upness seems more real than howdoyoudo mrs jones.

It does not seem to me possible there is anyone who has never leaped out of the future/past and into the world of what is. Just for an instant, at least. Afterward it was put aside for all sorts of reasons. It was too beautiful to be real. It was imagination: Nothing like that could exist. What would become of the children if I stayed there?

It was real.

The children would be better off.

Gene Gendlin was going to teach me *Focusing* over the telephone. The first time he did this he was at a weekend conference in San Francisco and he called on a Saturday. We reversed the charges for the telephone call and I was happily aware that the rates were a lot cheaper, as I was in Idaho. At the end of the session he suggested that we continue on Tuesday during daytime hours. I was still in Idaho—he would be in Chicago. I did a small gulp but my yes was definite. The thought of the telephone bill piling up was a bit unnerving, but worth it. For several weeks after that we had a non-weekend daytime session. Each time I had to put the cost out of my mind.

Last week he said when he called "Wouldn't this be a lot cheaper on Saturday?"

We have had a Saturday session ever since.

Why didn't *I* say in the first place "How about Saturday? It's a lot less expensive," or something similar?

I must not intrude on a professional man's private life. (Rule 1)

I must be grateful to him for teaching me Focusing and not ask for more. (Rule 2)

It might not be convenient for him to call on Saturday. (Rule 3—always consider the other person)

Probably there were some others lurking in the cobwebs of my mind that I didn't notice but they censored me out of existence just the same.

I could have asked, and accepted the answer whatever it was, and moved on from there.

Last fall I finished a book manuscript.

What I am writing now had occurred to me months ago.

I delayed writing it until I had seen the other book through to publication. I saw that. I mentioned it. There was no secret about it that I kept hidden from myself.

Or was there? I was unhappy and bored with my feeling of being stuck.

When I started the work in Focusing with Gene, my problem was my stuckness. Through Focusing I was released to writing this book, and then I saw how I had stuck myself. It was a Rule that had got between myself and action: Always finish one thing before you start another.

Ridiculous!

I burst out laughing.

Focusing seems to be a way to train my mind out of maya—the world of illusion. Conscious evolution.

At the time of my husband's suicide in Hawaii our son was nine years old. We were in Arizona. I told him that his father had died. When he asked me what his father had died of I wanted very much to tell him the truth but I knew that although intellectually I had accepted the suicide, below that was emotional turmoil which would surface in my voice if I spoke of it. Children pay more attention to the emotion in the voice than they do to the words. I answered his question by saying that I thought his father had died of unhappiness.

That was the truth and yet it wasn't. I suffered for many years—not continuously, but frequently and in an underlying way—because I hadn't been honest with him. By "years" I mean all through his finishing school and going to college and getting a job as a chemist. I wasn't free of it.

Then he needed his father's death certificate for something or other and I sent for a copy of it. When it came, it said how his father had died—by cutting his throat. I got the shakes and had to let myself shudder and moan so that I would be mostly calm when he came home from work and I told him. I said that I did not tell him at the time of his father's death because I was shaken and I felt that he was not in shape himself to handle it alone. He reflected on that, then said "I think you were right. I couldn't have taken it then."

There was absolutely nothing wrong with what I had done except my *belief* that I should have done otherwise. Incalculable strain and suffering of the kind that we dramatize on stage and screen and all of it totally unnecessary. Where did this notion come from? I don't know, but I think I had made a vow—to no one but myself—to be always honest with my son.

Another twenty-five years have passed since I told the truth and was absolved. I wrote about it here without distress. Then I began to cry a little, gently. Then I bawled—for probably half-an-hour, reminiscent of my childhood. My crying now was simply crying—nothing more. Relief. I didn't need someone to comfort me—crying was comfort enough.

I understand better my father's anger when I went to Arizona. I made it impossible for him to keep his vow to be responsible for me until I was twenty-one.

And it's *all* ridiculous!

A suicide is a person who has taken himself much too seriously. Big mistake. So is murder.

Surely this is my destination!
   Oh no, that is your stopover for tomorrow.

Azumi

Where did I get the notion that it must be *either* you *or* me?
I never thought of *both*. I spent a year trying to figure out
whether my husband or I was crazy. All that wasted
energy and time. When I got clear, it was obvious that we
were *both* crazy. In fact, all of us are but I didn't know
that then.

I have always had difficulty doing without an alarm clock.
I didn't wake up at the right time. The first time, I over-
slept and then next time I "corrected" to waking up at
midnight for a six o'clock start on the day. From then on
I was awake irregularly until five, after which I didn't
dare go back to sleep. Other people might have built-in
waker-uppers but I didn't—or else mine was permanently out of order.

   Pearl Harbor changed a lot of things. By piling up
stress on stress? In the week following the attack I was
alone with the children at night—my husband was on
duty at a first-aid station—and the military were expecting invasion on our side of the island. In fact, they
thought that Kaneohe which curved around the bay for
twenty miles was the most likely place for a landing. I
never did decide whether to wait for the Japanese to
come to us or to run for the mountains, but it seemed to
me that I should be alert to any sign of invasion. Staying
awake all night wouldn't do it. What would? It seemed to
me that if I woke up at two-hour intervals and looked
around that should be warning enough. Having made my
decision, I went to sleep.

One night at about one-thirty my nearest neighbor came up the hill to our house in search of comfort. She was lonely and afraid. We were all afraid but sometimes it got to us more than at other times.

After the first week some people said they hadn't been afraid but I didn't hear anyone say so at the time.

My neighbor told me about it next day. She said that she had banged and hollered and the two dogs with her had barked and she could see me through the window sleeping soundly, undisturbed.

If she had come up the hill at one of the times I had set to be awake I would have heard her step on the driveway even without the dogs. She just chose the wrong time for a visit. I wasn't there.

My unexpected talents have usually surfaced in moments of great stress and this led me to mistake the process. I thought that stress was necessary. This led me to think that if I could just be stressed sooner I could spare myself much agony.

Now it seems to me much more likely that the stress is followed by relaxation—like a rubber band that is stretched and when released it goes zong! and in that moment I am bright. I could get the same result by being relaxed in the first place.

Fact/fiction.

We don't seem to have made a lot of progress in the last sixty years toward recognizing the reality of fact/fiction: That in fact they are a fiction of our own making.

When I was seventeen, the Hollywood library had a sign saying "Histories of California removed to the fiction stacks."

I thought we were making progress.

In Berkeley a man grew a flourishing vegetable garden in a truck with no engine. The truck was in the street. He pushed the truck back and forth every 72 hours to comply with the law against over-parking. He did this for six months.

The city commissioners would have liked to give him permission not to move his vegetable garden every 72 hours but were afraid they might set a precedent. Suppose everyone started doing it?

I have heard three more times this month of people in different places who had an idea and were prevented from continuing it by the authorities who were afraid of the future.

Why not grant a license to the *first* one to do something—the innovator. Our streets might be much more interesting than they are. There's too much copying anyway. Monotonous.

Warren Bennis, then at MIT, liked the "circling nonlinear approach" of my writing in *Person to Person*. Non-Cartesian. Cartesian is the way for me *not* to go and Descartes for whom Cartesian was named is the man who said "I think, therefore I am." Also not for me.

I like Suzuki's *Agito ergo sum*. I don't vibrate much when my head is occupied with thinking.

Following straight lines shortens distances and also life.
Porchia

This book is more like life before I have assembled it into continuity. The trick is to let it assemble itself—and then do a vanishing act like the wake of a ship.

No hinting! Say what you mean.

I was pretty adamant about that. Just now I realized that it's a rule. I couldn't think of an instance in which it was binding. Puzzle. It is a rule to speak directly when you want something but how can that ever be bad? I used to say "No hinting!" to the children when that was obviously what they were doing. Like asking questions instead of saying what you want, frequently beginning or ending with "Don't you think?" but often sounding like a simple observation.

"There's quite a lot of chocolate cake that didn't get eaten last night." (I want a piece.)

"Norah's going skating tomorrow." (I want to go skating.)

"I don't think green looks good on me." (I want a new dress; she already has a green one.)

A friend was reading this. "It is *hinting* that is the rule," she said. "Whenever you say something directly, you do so without interference."

That's obvious to me *now!*

Did I make a mistake
    or did I mistook something?

When I am centered, psychological needs are non-existent. I don't need someone to keep me company, to sustain or support me, to do anything at all for me. No need. And my center, which had seemed so important to me, is gone—yet I feel no loss. Just one more piece of baggage that I thought I needed.

For years, I puzzled over this: When one woman did something stupid—like spilling the groceries all over the floor—and laughed at herself, I laughed with her. When another woman did the same thing, I didn't think it was funny. In fact, I didn't like *her*. So what went on? Did I approve something that someone did when I liked her, and disapprove when I didn't like her?

Mistook.

At long last, I was clear. When one person goofed and laughed, she wouldn't be likely to make the same mistake again. The other person was making a career of goofing. I didn't like her act.

Psychological memory creeps up on me stealthily, with ever more demands, ever more dependence, until the only way I can break with it is to make a break, which is better than not making it. Still, it is a rupture and takes time to heal.

Physical dependence exists. It isn't invented. Hiding behind a screen of money doesn't make it non-existent. It is impossible to escape. Even the man who lived alone high in the mountains had to come down sometimes for supplies and when he suicided he hanged himself with a rope he hadn't made.

Recognition of physical dependence or interdependence brings me closer to the garbageman, the millionaire, the farmer, the stewardess, the plants, the fish, the air, the sun, the clouds, the water . . .

I am part of the universe and the universe is me.

During World War I, when the Battle of the Marne was happening, I read the headlines in *The New York Times* over my father's shoulder and asked anxiously "Do you think we'll win?"

"Nobody wins a war," said my father. "Both sides make mistakes and the one that makes the most mistakes loses."

That may have been true. Now, everybody loses but we haven't caught on to that yet.

"You sound as if thinking is bad," said a man in the audience to the lecturer.

"It is," said Steve.

"To me, it is a wonderful gift," said the man.

"It is. Perhaps it's so recent in the evolutionary sense we haven't learned how to use it yet."

There is an old Spanish fable about a huge mirror that crashed on top of a mountain. The villagers who lived at the base of the mountain heard the noise and went trudging up the mountain to find out what had made the racket. Each one came upon a fragment of the mirror and exclaimed "I have found it!"

That's me.

I have always been at odds with the world in some respects—who isn't? It wasn't built with us in mind. What has been giving me difficulty now is the Over-way of the Western world while I try to follow the Under-way of the Eastern. Not that there aren't Westerners living the Eastern way and Easterners living the Western way and it is doubtful that anyone does anything 100 percent. But my problem is that I get in a jam when I push myself and the prevailing opinion (it prevails around me) is that I *should* push. Then everything would be all right. My eighty-year-old body protests being told to do more of what it has already done too much of. Too much rider whipping the horse along to get where *I* want to go. Not enough centaur.

Kezia and I are in the stationer's looking at pens. She tells me how wonderful these pens are and that she is going to purchase some more of them and so on and on. I have been using Flair Ultra Fine pens for years and am delighted with them but as she talks the image of another pen—image of an image, actually—comes into my mind. I pick up one of the new pens, then two . . .

These pens are very little used—just dutifully, to use them up. I don't like them as well.

I notice that Kezia is using a Flair pen now.

What was all the talking about?

There's no such thing as simultaneous.

There's too much space between.

I'm really getting cleaned up. I've been sitting on that one for twenty-five years. For six or seven years it's been on paper but the paper has gone sliding in and out of my life.

One morning I had partly left the dream state, partly was still in it, and I was looking at a very black sky with very white stars blinking in it. The words that accompanied this like a caption were the ones that I let stand on the previous page. No more shilly-shallying! This leaves time for something else or nothing. More and more I prefer nothing! It has more in it.

We make our own fortunes and we call them Fate, according to Disraeli. The role of victim never did appeal to me. Perhaps that's why I took matters into my own hands quite often: Nobody to blame but me.

But if you like the role of victim, that's all right. So is everything else.

He was only twenty years old. He had noticed that the things he worried about never happened. Solution: He worried about everything. When disaster befell from something that he hadn't thought of, he quickly added it to his list of things to worry about and faced the future with confidence.

M*ens sana in corpore sano.* How did I ever get hooked on that one? So *certain.*

A man with Parkinson's disease stayed—with his wife and two daughters—at a small hotel in Arizona. We saw him at meals, usually not otherwise. He did make a clatter as he undeftly manipulated the knife and fork against the plate.

One day as I passed his cabin I heard him calling, though a "call" is mistaken. It was more like a shrieking wail. I knew that his wife and children had gone for a drive, leaving him to take a nap. I called to him so he would know someone was coming, and entered the cabin without knocking when I got to it.

His speech was not reproducible but somehow I understood that his wife had been gone for more than an hour and he was worried about her. I knew the surrounding terrain and reassured him that it could easily take longer than anticipated. Then he asked me to help him get up. I told him I would if he could tell me what to do. He did. When we had got him with his knees over the edge of the bed, he held out his hands, which I took in mine and pulled him to his feet.

As he got to his feet, his bright eyes which I had not noticed twinkled at me and he said "That wasn't very difficult, was it?"

I had been so absorbed in trying to do the right thing the right way—which I need not have been since he was guiding me all the way—to be aware of him till then. Now I chuckle, remembering the delight of him. Which one of us was more sane? Personally, I vote for him.

Mens sana in corpore sano. Now why did I think for most of my life that meant that you can't have one without the other? It simply expresses an ideal.

This occurred to me this morning, several weeks after I had written about the man with Parkinson's. I have been alone for forty hours. What other corrections would make themselves if aloneness continued?

In aloneness I can hear myself more easily.

How much goes on in that quiet universe of which I know so little?

Who knows what is health or sane, anyway? It must have been said or written when some people thought they knew, like knowing the world is flat. Like me when I accepted it.

How good it feels to not know!

Reality!

In Hawaii at the time I lived there, there was a Hawaiian secretary of the Mormon church. I had lunch at his house one day. He broiled the chicken over an open fire just a little way from the open door of his house while his wife prepared the rest of the lunch just inside the door. I liked the chumminess of it. After lunch he took me to the Mormon Temple at Laie. He couldn't take me into the temple, of course, but he took me to the front door and we slowly walked around the building and as we walked he talked about The Book of Mormon. I was new to Hawaii at that time. Oh poor Hawaiians, I thought. Threw over their own idols and now they've got this? I didn't know that I didn't need to worry about them.

As we completed our tour and got back to the front door of the temple he said "Or so the story goes. Whether or not it is true, remains to be seen."

My husband was a good person who had been raised all wrong and as he was born in 1884 he hadn't had any of the modern tools to use to get out of it. His parents obviously didn't have them either. He was an improvement over his parents. This happens, but oh so slowly! We can speed up the process by becoming aware of wrongnesses and making them into rightnesses.

When we moved from New York to Hawaii (in 1934), he insisted on my preparing the road ahead so that it would be smooth and easy, a transition without a bump. As this isn't possible, it seems to me better to learn how not to feel the bumps.

I found a house to rent in Hanalei, Kauai, while we were living in New York. A friend of mine in Brooklyn was married to a sea captain and she had taken a trip with him that stopped in the Islands, where she met the wife of another sea captain... Eventually the trail led to what we wanted.

I asked the owner to have ice in the top of the ice box and food in the bottom for arrival more than a month later. I had quite a time finding out that we could go there by ship. The blocks to getting information were many—mostly the Matson Line—but we managed it and had a delightful dinner with a young man from the Grace Lines (which didn't go to Hawaii). If you start with the notion that something is possible, interesting things happen even if not what was originally intended.

What we took with us from New York was packed in a lift van—a huge box that gets hoisted onto the ship with a derrick. Thos. Cook & Son took our stuff from the apartment to somewhere else where they packed it. My husband figured it would take us six months to know where we wanted to live though how he figured that I don't know. He had it packed with enough mothballs or something else to keep out moths to guarantee safe storage for that long. He was sure that he understood these things from having lived in India. Along with the stuff that we actually used—his chair, bed, encyclopaedia table, bookcase, etc.—he also included a white enamel pail. Although our first residence had running water, he expected that we would be moving to a more primitive place. He was sure it could be used for carrying water. We never carried water. Neither did he ever play golf or wear his intern suits. Sometimes it seemed to me that he was prepared for all contingencies except what actually happened. In my view, there were people living in Hawaii with whatever was there and I could too. I took with me a small trunk.

The ship from Honolulu to Kauai—an overnight trip— docked at Lihue—where we took a taxi drive forty-five miles to Hanalei, beyond which there was nothing but cliffs dropping off to the sea. Happily we arrived at the house we had rented from New York. There was a slight hitch. The owner had put ice and food in the ice box but had forgotten to put a stove in the house. We were too happy to be bothered with that and went for a swim. Lolloping in the waves of Hanalei Bay, gazing at the ironwood trees which had previously been seen only in pictures, and at the sky which we had seen but never like this, we let the fatigue of travel ooze out of us.

Walking back from the beach to the house we saw something which we hoped wasn't there. A huge truck was parked in front of the house and on it was our lift van that was supposed to be put in storage in Lihue. Half a dozen smiling Hawaiians told us that they had seen our name on it and brought it to us on their way home. At the docks there was a hoist that could put the van on the truck. In Hanalei, there was nothing that would take it off. We hacked it open and distributed the stuff around the already furnished (except for a stove) house.

We forgot about the mothballs. All the windows of the house were open and usually our heads were hanging out of them, our stomachs uneasily aware of what they hadn't had for dinner.

Then the Japanese began practicing for the Bon dances. What a racket! Just as we were falling asleep at dawn there was a clatterbang of screeching mixed with noisy cans that were pulled with a string. The Chinese were scaring away the rice birds from the paddies.

We hadn't thought to bring ear muffs to Hawaii.

One of the loveliest expressions (to me) in pidgin English in Hawaii at the time I lived there, was "No can." The rural people used it freely. At first, to be sure, I was baffled. I would ask the yardman to trim the plants and he would say "No can."

I would ask a neighbor to go with me to the vegetable stand and she would reply "No can."

I would ask a child to run an errand for me and he would say "No can."

It left me with nothing to say. I couldn't argue with it because there was nothing to argue about.

That was the beauty of it!

It could mean I'm going to be somewhere else, I have to get the cane knife sharpened first, my grandmother will be buried tomorrow, I don't feel well, or even as it did quite often "I'm not in the mood," which was as acceptable as everything else.

Words are useful when they are useful and not when they're not.

Do you want to read what I have written?

No can.

There are so many different possible meanings that I give up trying to find which one is operative in this case. I get on with something else.

Sarah was visiting the Hawaiian Islands for the first time. She told me that she went to a beauty parlor in Waikiki to have her nails manicured.

Then she pondered the array of lipsticks for one that would match her new nails. When she finally selected one, the girl said "It costs seventy-five cents less at the drugstore down the street."

My friend exclaimed "For heaven's sake! Don't you want to sell your own stuff?"

"Certainly," was the reply. "But that's no reason for you to spend money if you don't want to."

My friend in search of a lipstick preferred to pay seventy-five cents more than to walk down the street to the drugstore. Her choice. Neutrality from the clerk who accepted it as what my friend wanted.

Dorothy was new to the Islands although she intended not to stay that way. The week before Easter she went into a florist's shop. She looked at all the lilies, then asked the owner how much they cost.

"More better buy Monday," said the man.

"Why is that?" she asked.

"Today two dollah half a dozen," said the man. "Monday fifty cents a dozen."

"I buy Monday," Dorothy told him.

The seller of flowers nodded. Dorothy nodded and departed with an appreciation of the ease and friendliness of it—giving information and letting her make the choice.

Do you have scissors? I asked the clerk.

Only very terrible ones, she answered.

I bought them. They were just what I wanted.

Awareness is very puzzling if you haven't yet got the hang of it. I'm not sure that I have. Awareness of *what?* What is the meaning of *total* awareness? Quite possibly I am one of the blind men who described the elephant according to whether he had got hold of the trunk, a leg, or some other part of its anatomy. But this I know: From my ignorance I say that awareness is like the top of the mountain from which you can see all around. I have had my nose to the ground so much of my life, rooting around like a hog looking for truffles and that—the way I did it—is not awareness.

Everything in the world—the universe—is changing, including me.

I only wish I did it faster faster faster. I know it wants to happen and in spite of myself I hold it back with *my* bodymind.

I knew that once, by observation, and forgot it again. I was so stuck . . . that seems to deny my earlier statement, that everything changes. If I have been changing how can I be stuck? A paradox is only a paradox until I have got above it and seen that it is no paradox at all. Sort of like swinging in a hammock, then swinging so high that I hit the branch I'm hanging from and from there can see what is happening down below.

There was a time when I was learning a bunch of lies like how to be a good wife, a good mother, a good member of the community. (If you are doing those things you have my blessing. I have no wish to change what you're doing. You also have my blessing any time you choose to give it up.)

It took Pearl Harbor to blast me out of what I was in. Everything I had lived by got shot to hell and there seemed to be nothing to hold me together. But there was. There always is. That's not a mouthing of what someone has said but my own knowing.

For several years I could see no sense in that senseless slaughter and to tell me that I would someday be grateful for it would have seemed nonsense. But I am.

It may not be necessary for you. It was for me.

About a year after the revolution in Cuba, young Castro said "Having a revolution is certainly different from thinking about having one."

I was impressed. But what isn't different from thinking about it?

We had decided to move to Hawaii nine years before we could do it. In the meantime, I used the Forty-Second Street Library to look up Hawaii and read everything I could about it. We got in touch with a distributor of films and he notified us whenever there were newsreels of Hawaii being shown. We went haring off to anywhere in Manhattan, Brooklyn, the Bronx, or Queens to see them. I became so fluent in Hawaiiana that when I sat next to a man at dinner who had spent some time in the Islands, instead of questioning him I talked with him as though I too had been there. Then I said something about Lumahai where the hala trees seemed to be always blowing and he said, with a touch of embarrassment, "I don't know the place. You see, I only lived there for six months."

When we got to Hawaii, I was stunned. It was hardly as I had expected it to be. Ten thousand things seemed to be different, which changed the picture as a whole. I had to keep revising what I thought I knew about Hawaii.

The same can be said of other things I got into. Like marriage. Like having children. They weren't at all what I had expected. I felt slaughtered, over and over, and I didn't see that what had been slaughtered was nothing but an *idea*—a *fantasy*—an *illusion*—although it hurt like a knife in my chest. I had made a picture in my head—it existed nowhere else—and then screamed when it was ripped apart.

Laughable, no?

When we lived in Hawaii, the Big Five companies ran just about everything. This was good or evil according to which side you were on. I was on both.

The companies had interlocking directorates and functioned as a co-operation. This had the "bad" feature of keeping prices high but I'm not sure it wasn't worth the price. Who was it said "Buy less, enjoy more." Go into any store in town and ask for something. If they didn't have it, they told you at which store you could get it, or they would say there was none in the Islands.

Shopping became something to be moved about in easily while enjoying the walk, the wind, the sunshine and the rain, the faces and gestures of people.

No burden.

We lived in the country. I came home from a day's shopping in Honolulu refreshed.

When the Koolaupoko Improvement Club was successful in keeping unwanted improvements out of the twenty-mile stretch of Koolaupoko, the Big Five companies took advantage of our loose organization—no membership lists, for one thing. They asked if one of their members could address the club. We agreed, more out of politeness than interest, and stipulated that a vote would be taken on what they proposed at the following meeting. On the evening when the member was to speak, there were three or four times as many people present as usual, the newcomers brought in especially for the occasion by the Big Five. The proposal was that our club join the group of clubs around the Island that we called the Sewing Circle. At the end of the meeting it was voted—by all those present, of course—to have a vote on the proposal that evening, and then that proposal was voted on. All the king's men outvoted us. By the end of the meeting we had disbanded and become part of the Sewing Circle.

It seemed to me sad. But nobody went to the Sewing Circle! I was enchanted to notice as I went around enjoying my day that the same people were getting together out of their common interest—spontaneously, not deliberately—and something else was forming, like petals opening into a flower.

In wartime Honolulu there were sloughs of jobs but no place to live. Full up everywhere. One man offered me a job as cashier in a restaurant at some fabulous salary "and more if you don't rob the till." I couldn't take it because I had nowhere to live. The restaurant owner told me he was sorry he couldn't buy a house for me but he had bought three houses for cashiers and then they quit the job and kept the houses. He couldn't afford any more houses.

A house a house my kingdom for a house. How could I find some place to live? We had to leave the Alexander Young Hotel by the end of the week because that was all they allowed. If they hadn't set a limit they would have been full of permanent guests.

Who had a place to live?

Ah! There were a number of people who were holding the maid's quarters for the servants they couldn't get now that there was war work for everyone.

That is how I landed a job as cook in a small boarding house and had two rooms and bath in a garden and within walking distance of the school that Steve was going to. Every night I got through work about eight o'clock. I would have liked to have more evening to myself and my son so I tried to hurry. I *did* hurry. And every evening I got through work—finished the last dish—ten minutes *later*.

I told this to Jim Klee, then a professor of psychology at Brandeis University, and he told me that he had made the same observation: He walked to school, and on those days when he hurried, it took longer.

In the Koolaupoko Improvement Club when something was suggested that others found appealing they said *Kokua*. Their meaning was "I'll go along with that in any way I can." That doesn't mean that I'll break my back getting signatures or I'll shove something else out of my life in order to do this or I'll exert myself to squeeze this in somehow or you can count on me to get *results*.

The word is not important. The meaning is. We don't have a way to say it briefly: In the course of my daily life I'll forward this idea whenever an opportunity presents itself.

No burden. No sacrifice of life.

I went to Western Samoa because when it had been an independent nation for two years the UN gave it special commendation for the way it had conducted itself "without recrimination for past colonialism or present independence." I wanted to know what made that possible. I found out. Everybody makes mistakes so these are not held against them. I made many mistakes in Western Samoa and was glad to know this.

There was a small airline that ran between Apia and Pago Pago. There was a lot of ocean in between. The two pilots made their own decision whether they would take off, each trip. It was the rainy season when we were there.

One pilot was Australian, the other a New Zealander. We were talking about competition and the Australian said "You've *got* to have competition." The New Zealander said quietly "I'm not competitive. I just do a good job."

When the weather was stormy, the Australian pilot kept going out on the hotel veranda and looking at the sky, obviously ill at ease.

When it was the New Zealand pilot's turn he came out on the veranda, looked at the sky, and either took a taxi to the airport or went back to his room.

Louise pointed to her eye and said she had been using a hammer when the head of the nail she was hammering flew off and hit her near the eye, nicking the flesh. She said it with a touch of wailing.

"How lucky that it didn't hit your eye," I said.

She looked/sounded puzzled as she said "That was my first thought."

A miss is as good as a mile. I heard that so often as a child from my mother and her half-Irish family. It sure is.

It's okay to be dramatic if that's your preference, as long as you don't get lost in your performance.

In Chile I remarked to a young man at lunch that it's lucky the human fetus is worn on the inside because if it were worn on the outside no one would be able to resist giving it a pinch here or a twirl there to make it more to their own liking. The young man's first child was just two weeks old and out of his adoration he said "Oh no!" and then began talking to the people on his right while I resumed talking with the people on my left.

After a while he turned to me and said with rueful honesty "I *would* like to change the nose."

When we had Gestalt groups at Shura, Steve sometimes had people take a fantasy trip and sometimes I was one of the people. One of the fantasies was that of going into a pawnshop that had everything in the world in it and you could take whatever you wanted. Then, when you had made your selection and were about to leave the shop, you had to give something in return to the man who runs the shop.

I forget now what I took from the shop but I can't forget—not that I want to!—that when I came to the man I said "There's only one thing I want to give you and I can't bear to give you that."

"What is it?" he asked.

"All the words and thoughts in my head."

"Oh," he said, "that's nothing. Give them all to me any time." His gestures said that I could pour them in whenever I liked and he would let them float off into nowhere. "They're nothing," he said again.

I saw them then as a lot of vapors that take no space and disperse easily, leaving nothing behind. What a relief!

Thinking does get in the way, I thought, then boshed myself for thinking—which is another thought.

Some of the nicest, least-expected things happen when somebody doesn't show up and those who do haven't got their heads set on what was supposed to happen.

When I went to Maui because of the difficulties with my husband, I knew that I had to get out of what I was in to see clearly. I don't know if the same was true of my son. I do know that he began talking—not a lot but devastatingly when he did—in a way that he hadn't before. "The way Dad looks at me is like an iron bean in my heart."

It was clear to me then that we must not go back to living with his father. I wrote and told him so.

After that, one letter from him said that we MUST go to the mainland, and the next one said that we COULDN'T go to the mainland, and the next that we MUST go to the mainland and the next that we COULDN'T go to the mainland—and repeat. I was so geared to trying to please him that I was trying to figure out which he wanted. It was much too long before I saw that I couldn't do what he wanted because he didn't know what that was.

And that forced us into doing what *we* wanted to do.

What a gift!

That's the best decision I ever unmade!

I was at a t'ai chi workshop with Chungliang Al Huang. An engineer, newcomer to what was then called the human potential movement, was very troubled about his three children who were not children any more. "I used to be able to tell them what they should do. Now, I don't know."

"Why not tell them that you don't know?"

His laughter boomed in the room, outside the room, and back again like a boomerang. "I never thought of that!"

This is the way I see it now: Here is this child. It is in interaction with this world in all its aspects that it develops whatever way it does. *Inter*-action: Mutual or reciprocal action or influence. The *child* plays its part in all this. I saw this as a child though then I did not have the words to say it. There was an enlarged photograph in our living room of a chubby smiling baby on a bearskin rug. That was my sister. There wasn't one of me which I understood was because I wouldn't have made a pretty picture and the adults had other things on their minds. A smiling baby produces smiles.

I was not a smiling baby. As my uncle Bob said neutrally when I was old enough to remember, "You sure cried a lot when you were a baby." I weighed four pounds three ounces and my mother wailed "A four-pound chicken is just nothing." I was first put in an incubator and then given to my father to die as that is what I was doing anyway. My mother was still in the hospital because she had peritonitis. To think that these events didn't give both my parents a shaking up—perhaps equivalent to my shaking up by Pearl Harbor—is ridiculous. The world that I was born into was not only six years different from that of my sister. I was born into a different scene, and I was a different character.

This interaction with the world may be good or bad and usually it is both in varying degrees and according to who is looking at it and *when*. The child brings upon itself just as the adult brings upon itself and what it brings upon itself depends partly on the adult's(s') response(s) to what the child does which depends partly on what the child does which depends partly on what the adult does and . . .

I think we need a new approach entirely.

How do I raise a child—when my dream for the child does not match my husband's dream for the child and neither of them takes into account the child's dream for himself?

Answer: Stop dreaming.

Harry Bone, eminent psychologist and member of the William Alanson White Psychiatric Institute, told me that he was living alone when his mother moved in with him. This was never good and it became so bad it was intolerable. He told his mother that she would have to leave. She refused to go. After further suffering Harry decided that *he* would have to go, full of imaginings of what his mother would say. What she did say was totally unexpected.

"At *last* I can live my own life."

In Australia a woman told me of her relief when her fifteen-year-old daughter left home. "A mother can't throw out her own child," she said.

At Lake Cowichan a couple of young women wandered in. They were only there for an hour or two. They talked of how badly they had behaved as teenagers until at last they had been thrown out. They had lacked the courage to throw themselves out.

All that stress and suffering over nothing. What a waste. All tangled up with maya, the world of illusion. Nobody doing easily what they wanted to.

Why shed tears? It's *very* funny.

136

Vivekananda said a mother should be like a good governess who cares for the children and when they no longer need her puts on her hat and goes off to another job. I liked the sound of that but was already trapped by what we all are trapped by: What other people think. *Other* people? How can I be trapped if I don't think it myself?

Big Me getting in the way again.

A group of adults were talking about things that had been done to them all wrong by their mothers. I said to my ex-son who was one of the adults, "I don't *think* I ever did that to you. Did I?"

And he said "No! And it's given me a lot of trouble!"

Praise is used as a way to manipulate people. "You do this *so well*," one boss repeatedly told me in order to get me to do willingly the jobs that he didn't want to do himself.

"You're a wonderful manager!" my husband told me when he wanted me to manage something for him.

Teachers (all kinds, including parents) use praise to make good students go on being good students when it would be better for them to be worse.

My mind is blank when I try to find examples of when I did the same thing but that doesn't mean I didn't do them.

I remember clearly when I dumped praise, and pride.

"You must be very proud of your son."

I wasn't. I was purely happy.

In New Zealand's glow worm caves all the tourists got in small boats that were propelled by the boatmen latching onto hooks in the roof of the cave. They explained to us the necessity for keeping silence. If we didn't the glow worms wouldn't glow.

Gad it was lovely! Just the soft swish of the water as the boats moved along and the little glow worms glowing overhead.

Ted was a young man who went to college and stayed there until he noticed that all the others were there because they didn't know what else to do and he was there for the same reason. He went to work for the Forest Service blazing trails in mountainous country. He said he didn't understand the way the rest of the team worked. "They attack the brush with such force—and then sit down and puff and pant. Then they fight it again—sit down and rest again." He demonstrated their actions with his body and then his own way which was ease-y, was t'ai chi, nothing but flowing movement, swinging and returning without a break. Strength without force. "I don't have to rest," he said. "I can do that all day."

And he did.

In teaching t'ai chi, Chungliang Al Huang said "You put your foot down gently because you don't know what's there—maybe it's grass, maybe it's water." As I did this I felt an easing throughout my body which had not been there when I thought I knew, as if I had shifted gears. Awareness came in of its own accord—without my seeking. It was nice to feel this ease—instead of leading with my head.

A woman exclaimed "I'm so full of energy I don't know what to do with it!"

"That's not energy—that's tension," Chungliang Al told her.

"How would you describe energy?" I asked.

He looked thoughtful for a moment then "Like little fishes swimming," he said.

Here's another one that I've been keeping to myself and even now I whisper it softly:

Nothing makes any sense but the sense we make of it.

Now I'll probably find out that many people have made the same observation. Welcome!

Right away comes confirmation!
  Paul came back from a river trip laughing.
  On the river, one person said "You get what you need."
  Another person said "You get what you deserve."
  Person three said "You get what you get."
  I chuckle.

Science and Religion are both much like children of whom
  too much is expected.

There was once a chicken who got transferred to a new
home. She was cautious and when the farmer came to
feed the chickens once each day, she hid until the farmer
had gone. Only then did she come out to eat. She did this
100 times and at last had confidence. She didn't hide
when the farmer came with the food. The farmer grabbed
her and wrung her neck.
  She is called the Scientific Chicken.

  The moral I get from this story is that if I waited for
Science to approve everything before I did it, the chances
of getting my head chopped off are about equal.

You see, one thing is, I can live with doubt and uncertainty and not knowing. I think it's much more interesting to live not knowing than to have answers which might be wrong. I have approximate answers and possible beliefs and different degrees of certainty about different things. But I'm not absolutely sure of anything and there are many things I don't know anything about, such as whether it means anything to ask why we're here, and what the question might mean. I might think about it a little bit and if I can't figure it out, then I go on to something else. But I don't have to know an answer. I don't feel frightened by not knowing things, by being lost in a mysterious universe without having any purpose, which is the way it really is, so far as I can tell possibly. It doesn't frighten me.

Richard P. Feynman

When I don't know my way I have to find it by using whatever information I have—there's always *some*—by moving tentatively, step by step, by *noticing* and responding to whatever happens.

Then it's a romp whether I'm starting a business or finding out about swamis.

Short form. For the long form see *Person to Person*.

I wanted to take a painting on the plane from Oakland not many years ago. It was too big to go under the seat. I tried all the usual sources of information—airlines, travel agents, and the places they referred me to—to find out if this was possible. Nobody had any answers for me but one man did say that the reason he couldn't say was that it was up to the individual who checked the tickets at the gate. I had a place to begin.

I went to the gate with everyone else when they began admitting people, carrying the painting on the far side from the agent. He checked my ticket without noticing. I went through the gate. I was considerably past him when he noticed and came after me, saying "Nothing can be taken aboard that won't fit under the seat!" I nodded, to indicate that I had heard him, and continued walking. He hesitated, then came after me again and said much the same thing. I nodded and continued walking.

The agent looked back at the line of people waiting to have their tickets checked and literally threw up his hands and went back to them.

A little man who had been talking to me in the waiting room came up from the rear and told me, helpfully, that there was more space under the two seats in the center of the plane. Yes, but not enough for the painting I had carried on board. A stewardess looked at it and threw up her hands in many directions as she said maybe at the back, no there was something else there, maybe—no—she didn't know where to put it—acting out frenzy and frustration quite alarmingly.

Then the other stewardess appeared, sized things up at a glance, and put the painting in the clothes closet.

There's always someone and one is all I need.

When I was leaving Chile there was a fantastically long walk from the gate to the plane. I had covered half of it when I heard my name called and turned to see who it was. A man and a woman came toward me bearing gifts.

"We were late," said one of them, "and the gate was closed. We didn't know what to do. Then we remembered what you told us and we walked past the guard."

There are no rules. There are only exceptions.
                                              Ryuho Yamada

Moab, Utah, isn't near anywhere, according to *Time Magazine*. We lived forty miles beyond Moab in a small isolated valley. We had no telephone. When Steve said he would come on a certain day, he always came either on that day or the next. When he didn't come on the second day, Susan and I deliberately thought of everything possible to account for it. We really pushed the possibilities—and they *were* possibilities—thinking of another one approximately every minute until we wore down and eventually out. We couldn't think of another one.

When Steve did arrive several days later, the reason he hadn't come on schedule was something we hadn't thought of—not only that, but we *couldn't* have thought of.

That was helpful to me in letting go and waiting to see what happened. By then it is too late to get excited.

I'm not sure if spontaneity can be intentional but I think so, if you deliberately provide the right conditions for it to happen. When Steve was working at Shell Chemical he was so bored and I was so bored living in Torrance which seemed to me an awful place at that time. We did a lot of things to relieve the boredom. He wrote poetry and twisted reality into loops and fooled his superiors at work in ways they didn't recognize although sometimes they were puzzled. I practiced drawing with my left hand, sent a bunch of pages of manuscript to half a dozen men asking them what they got out of it. Each got something, none got the same thing, and only one of them was close to what I thought I had written. This was an eye-opener.

Steve and I mutually practiced spontaneity.

Shell Chemical disapproved an employee who even thought of leaving the company (at that time—I don't know about now) so when Steve decided that he wanted to study psychology in Abe Maslow's department at Brandeis he had to lie to get off from work to take the graduate record exams. One evening he ran through a bunch of lies experimentally. After that he said nothing more about it. When he went off on the day of the exams, I didn't know what he had told his boss.

He had expected to be back at work at two o'clock. At half-past two the phone rang. It was his boss, I was reasonably sure, although he did not introduce himself. He asked for John Stevens.

I said as slowly as possible, to give myself time to empty my head of all the thoughts that came into it, that he wasn't there—the only conceivable answer when I couldn't produce him.

"Is this his mother?" he asked, almost demanded.

Y-e-s-s. (Same motive.)

(Sounding as though he had caught Steve in a lie, which of course he had): "He said he had to take you to the doctor!"

(Same pace, unperturbed.) "He did, but afterward he had to take a prescription to the pharmacy."

"Oh, never mind, here he comes now," he said and hung up.

When Steve got home that evening I asked him how he had explained his being late and he said "I told him that I had to get a prescription filled."

Love without an object has always been the most cherished love I know.

When my son was looking for a mate, I told him "I hope that you'll find someone who has faith." I knew completely what I meant. Not faith *in* something or someone—just faith. Now I know that it was faith without an object that I had in mind. Objects tend to let you down. Faith without them can't be extinguished.

So that makes two no-objects. I noticed very recently that my thoughts were without an object (at that time). Not hitched to anything. Floating free.

And then that I was smiling without an object.

So that makes four. How many else are there?

Everything?

What happens to the subject when there is no object?

Merleau-Ponty says if I take my right wrist in my left hand, my wrist is the object and my left hand is the subject.

If I then pick up a piece of paper with my right hand, the paper becomes the object and the right hand the subject. Shifty business.

But if I put my hands with palms together—no subject, no object. Both disappear.

I still have hands.

"**D**on't answer the question. *Ask* it."

Krishnamurti's frequent repetition of those words didn't mean a thing to me until I tried it. Then I learned something. I get a different answer—a refreshingly new answer—when I do this. It comes from a different place.

It is a way of booting intellect out of first place and getting in touch with something that makes better sense. I hesitate to call *it* anything. But *it* has certain qualities that I wish for more of—flexibility, non-duality, more and better information.

I can't make it clear to myself or you with words.

*"**D**on't bite my finger, look where I am pointing."*
Warren McCullough

If I don't know what to do, I do nothing. Absolutely nothing. Then inwardly I am completely silent—not seeking, not pursuing—there is no center at all. Then I know love that is without an object, that can never become hate or anger even momentarily, although I may slip back into duality.

Cut the high-fallutin gabble, gal. A small boy was asked "What do you do when you think?"

After a couple of false starts he said "You just stand still and don't do nothing and something comes into your brain."

I became aware that I was blocking myself. I didn't know what to do about it.

Before my eyes—behind them, actually, although I'm not sure just how vision takes place—I saw an image of a brick wall with here and there some water seeping through.

> pink/red bricks
> white/grey mortar
> green/blue water seeping slowly through like tiny
> sluggish waves.

I let go my muscles, taking my clue from the one infallible advisor. No doubt at all. No question. Nothing to be said but yes.

Right away I wanted more! If only the organism that is/is-not me would advise me more often, living life would be so simple. No doubting.

A moving picture raced along behind my forehead showing me that the thought I'd had that had preceded the movie wasn't true.

All I needed to know was a brick wall with water seeping through.

                    duality:
work   play
              split

                    plerk:
not this   not that
              both and neither
                  no split
              beyond duality

        where I and me and you get together with none
                    of us present

Three Bowmen
a fable by Avery Johnson

The king called for a great archery contest and all the archers in the land came, hoping to participate in it. When they gathered around to hear more about the contest, the king announced that there would be some special conditions imposed: The bows and arrows used would not be the ones familiar to the contestants but would be supplied to them from the arsenal of the king's bowmaker. Furthermore, there would be only one day to practice and prepare for the event.

Just one day! No one could learn to use a new bow in one day! Many of the archers shook their heads and withdrew from the list. When those who still wanted to compete went to the arsenal to make their selections from the new and unfamiliar equipment, they saw that there was a great variety to choose from in the design of the bows and that all were very different from anything that they had ever seen or used before. This would indeed be a challenge. More archers now turned away and there were but three remaining.

One of the best in the land was named Xakto and he stepped forward to choose a bow. Xakto was known for his precise and methodical approach to everything he did. Naturally he selected a bow which had on it every kind of sighting aid and leveling and counterbalancing gadget one could possibly imagine. There also came with it a very complete operator's manual. Xakto headed for the practice range with a bunch of arrows and a target that was simply a small black spot on an otherwise unmarked surface.

The second contestant to step forward was Striver, whose approach was more sporting. He chose a simpler bow with a counterweight for comfort and a small, fixed sighting arrangement on it so that he could at least be consistent in where he thought he was aiming. Along with his bow and arrows, he took with him a target that was the usual bull's eye. The entire target was large enough so that he thought he ought to be able to land an arrow on it somewhere with even his earliest shots. Off he went, to begin practicing.

Last came Zendor, a strongly built youth from somewhere in the countryside. He was smiling and relaxed as he called for one of the children who were watching the proceedings to come forward to make his selection for him. "Choose the bow that pleases your eye and your hand the most, then let me find out if it also pleases mine. Take all the time you need." The child looked at the bows and felt them all and finally she picked up the one that she had found herself going back to look at and to touch again because it had a peculiarly pleasing wood grain and shape and smoothness. When she handed it to Zendor, he smiled and readily agreed that that was the one for him. He picked up a handful of arrows and started for the practice range, whereupon the king asked "Aren't you going to select a target to practice with?"

"Oh," said Zendor, "it doesn't really much matter what I shoot at. I'll use this large rug that I carry around with me. Its colors and patterns are pleasing to me and I can drape it over a fence or a wall or the branch of a tree. It will do for me quite well, thank you."

When they reached the practice range, Xacto was already making ready to quit for the day. He looked somewhat tired and cross. His body was tensed from having stood rigidly for so long with each shot, waiting until all the sight-lines and levels and gauges were in their right places before releasing the arrow. He had done this several times, making adjustments in the bow's instrument after each shot. On his target there were a number of arrows at various distances from the center spot and just one arrow in that spot—his last shot. He considered himself ready and on the following day he would win by reason of his invincible precision, along with his ability to stand like a rock until every instrument settled into its proper reading.

Striver was still practicing. Every time he would shoot an arrow and it landed in one of the target's rings, he would groan and comment miserably on the amount by which he had missed the center spot. A few of the arrows had landed there and Striver had left those in place to remind himself that success was possible, if not yet very frequent. He knew that he must try and try and *try* and that eventually all of his suffering and bad shooting would diminish as he gained proficiency with this new bow. He was totally immersed in the agony of trying. Each time he did manage to hit the bull's eye his pain gave way to optimism, but only until the next shot. He found it difficult to figure out what combination of corrections was working right for him when he did strike the center, but he hoped to be able to master it before tomorrow.

Zendor looked around for a good place to practice so that he would also be able to enjoy the surrounding view and so that the spectators would be comfortable and not have the sun in their eyes. He found a suitable tree branch for spreading his rug upon and everyone saw that it was a tapestry decorated with a lovely mixture of geometrical patterns and flowers and leaves and vines. There certainly didn't appear to be any "center" to it but it was enjoyable just to let one's eyes wander over it and come to rest here and there as one pleased.

Zendor picked up the bow and an arrow, looked at them care-fully, and felt them all over. He seemed to pay scant attention to his target but looked instead at the crowd and smiled. He gazed at the view and at the clouds and at the grasses waving in the breeze. He stretched himself a little and then, almost in one motion, he nocked the arrow, drew back the bow, and let fly. Heaven knows where his eyes were at that moment! It didn't seem to matter to him. After the arrow landed he looked at where it was sticking into his rug and said aloud "Aha! *That's* where I was aiming!" Again he went through the same relaxed procedure but somehow not quite in the same way, and again looked at where the arrow had gone and exclaimed "Well, well, *that's* where I was aiming that time."

And so it went. Zendor appeared to be enjoying himself as much as anyone and kept up the practicing for hours while talking to the bystanders about the contest and the weather and about their own lives and troubles. It was difficult to guess whether Zendor was gaining proficiency with his new bow but it didn't seem to matter to him. He was so relaxed about what he was doing that it was hard to imagine that he was practicing anything. The only noticeable change was that toward the end of the day he took a little longer between the drawing back of the bowstring and the release of the arrow. On the last few dozen shots his smile was broader than it had been earlier and he finished up the day with the placement of six arrows in a neat pattern around one of the leaves pictured on the rug. It was a surprising gesture.

One lad, Stochastos, who had been watching, was curious to know what kind of practicing this was that Zendor had been doing and he offered to carry Zendor's rug so that he could walk along with him and ask about it.

"Well," said Zendor scratching his chin, "at first I just don't pay much attention to where the arrows go. How can I know all of the many thousands of factors that go into each shot? That's too much for my poor head to handle. I'd much rather enjoy the day and the people around me."

"But," asked Stochastos, "surely in the contest tomorrow you aren't going to shoot your arrows just anywhere?"

"No, no," said Zendor. "They'll go where I want them to go. You see, after I've been shooting awhile, I can begin to guess where each arrow is going to land and, as time goes on, my guesses have a feeling more like knowing. By the end of the day, I find I can choose a new point on the rug each time and I wait with the bow drawn until a feeling comes to me that says 'Now!' and I release the arrow. It's the best way I know not to get in the way of whatever it is that I'm learning. It's funny how 'trying hard' is like failing. It's something you want to get rid of. I'd rather work with something that *grows*. Now this bow is like a part of me and I also know that the same feeling of 'Now!' will return to me tomorrow during the contest."

On the next day the three bowmen and a great crowd of spectators arrived at the archery range in eager anticipation of the event. The king stood up and announced that he had one more set of conditions to impose upon the contestants. He apologized for not having been able to announce these conditions on the previous day but to do so would have defeated their purpose. "Above all else," he said, "what I want is to reward the ability to be flexible and to respond to novelty. The circumstances of this contest have to be new and unexpected.

"Each of you," the king continued, "will shoot three arrows and each one of them in a different way. The first you may shoot in a manner of your own choosing and taking as much time as you desire."

All three bowmen nodded and the king went on. "Just before you are handed your second arrow, a bag will be dropped over your head so you can no longer see the target. Take the arrow and shoot as soon thereafter as you can."

At this new and bizarre development Xakto turned pale then flushed and walked away shaking his head. Never had he heard of such an unreasonable condition! He would not compete in this strange contest.

"For the third shot," said the king, "the target will be caused to swing on a giant pendulum, but you may shoot when and as you please."

At this point Striver wanted to drop out too but his friends urged him to give it his usual Grand Try—there was nothing to lose by it.

The outcome?

Zendor knew that he had hit the mark without even having to look.

And here is a final paradox. All those who have tried to express the experience of the pure Now have found language to be woefully inadequate. "The Tao that can be expressed is not the real Tao," wrote Lao Tzu 2500 years ago. When Master Shin-t'ou was asked to explain the ultimate teaching of Buddhism, he answered "You won't understand it until you have it."

Paul Watzlawick

First I have to let in the problem—stop denying it. Recognition. After that I can begin to work on it. The evidence that I am crazy is as obvious as the clear blue sky up there today. Would anyone who wasn't crazy spend so much time complicating his life in ten thousand different ways which are all one way? And then complain that *life* is so difficult? That in itself is crazy!

More than a year ago, Anthony went over the manuscript of this book with an editoral eye. He marked a bunch of pages *preachy*. I looked at the words on paper and into myself. I couldn't find anything preachy. I did this repeatedly. I tortured myself (mildly) looking for my preachiness—which I was sure was there so I must be hiding it from myself. I asked a number of people if they found it preachy and they didn't. Still, if Anthony had found it, it must be there.

Another editor recently read the manuscript and I asked him if he found any of it preachy. He said no.

At last I did what I should have done in the first place— asked Anthony what he meant by *preachy*. He replied (and I burst out laughing) "Your not thinking of what 'preachy' means to me is part of what I mean by being preachy—using words that do not connect to specific experiences in the listener/reader. The words can mean anything to anyone—good for winning elections or inducing trance, but not so good for communciation."

I never dreamed that he, or anyone, had that meaning of *preachy* in his head. The dictionary doesn't include it. I think *political* would be more likely to be understood than *preachy*, although this is no closer to the dictionary definition.

The problem of words. I don't know what to do about it but be aware—aware that words mean different things to different people—and this makes me tentative. Not hesitant—that's different (to me)—but tentative, aware that I may not know what the other means, and if it's important to me, ask.

Or, don't look for other people's answers in yourself.

The sin of permanence. To think of permanence is a mistake because nothing is. When you cling to something that isn't, your arms wear out.

When you aren't living with reality, you get bumped and sometimes dumped.

The seminar with Tarthang Tulku Rinpoche, Tibetan lama, began with Friday evening supper at Nyingma Institute in Berkeley. All meals were silent—that is, without talking. At each meal we sat down and waited for Rinpoche to come in and sit at his table. We chanted with him. After that, supper began.

Some of us didn't know these customs or forgot them. I put my napkin in my lap right after I sat down. Old habit. Later I softly asked the man next to me to pass the tea. No rebukes, no disapproving glances, no instructions. I heard all our mistakes clear gently. At supper they were like the rippling of a brook. At breakfast, the brook was more quiet. At lunch I heard it only now and then. By Saturday evening supper, the brook had reached still waters. I discovered that asking someone for what I wanted was unnecessary. Without the chatter we were more observant. Someone notices that there's no (vegetable) lasagna on a neighbor's plate and offers it. When I move my hand toward a platter I cannot reach, someone picks it up and puts it in my hand.

At the beginning of each meal, we waited for Rinpoche. At the end of each meal, he waited for us. When every last sound and movement of eating had stopped, he rose and left. We did likewise. Obviously I am writing about what *was*. I have heard that this is not the same at all seminars and that each time what Rinpoche does in the seminars is different. When something is always done in the same way, soon I do it that way like an automaton. Awareness is lost. Besides, physical circumstances change, and I must change to be in accord with them.

There were small printed leaflets saying what we would do, when. This was more or less followed. The "less" was a bother to some people. They were distressed that what happened wasn't always what they had in their heads—taken from the printing. It didn't exist anywhere else. The subject announced for the weekend was Kum Nye Relaxation. I expected a Method. I don't know if what Rinpoche did with us was The Method. It seemed to me to be more in the direction of breaking up methods, or perhaps a sampler of many exercises that are all part of the method. He led us in some yoga exercises, switching to a different one before we had the hang of what we were doing. He lay on the floor with his head propped against the wall as he instructed us in something or other. He guided us in self-massage. He gave us some instructions for meditation which we followed for a short while. My thin hands were becoming plump and soft and gentle. I wanted to go on with that. We moved on to something else—not hurriedly, but nonetheless moving on.

Rinpoche led us in chanting several times during the sessions. Once, that switched to clapping. People were smiling and laughing. I don't know how that happened. Either I missed something or I have forgotten it.

Once, when we were chanting, Rinpoche said to let the sound of our emotions come through. I do this sometimes. I feel good doing it and afterwards am more at ease. This morning I started chanting. Afterward I noticed that while I was hearing the sounds, aware of the vibrations in my body, the relaxing of my jaw muscles, I didn't think. Nice vacation. Later, when I was reading and writing, I noticed that all my past mistakes were gone and my future ones hadn't happened yet. Blessed interlude!

This was my first experience of meditation. Rinpoche said to look at a point two feet away. He said to do this with soft eyeballs. I had wondered about that aspect of meditation—looking at something or nothing for a long time. Staring is not good for eyes. Muscles need flexibility to function well.

What I learn in a special situation is no good to me unless it becomes a part of my everyday life. Otherwise it's like going to church on Sunday and forgetting the whole thing the rest of the week. A friend of Chungliang Al Huang's studied judo so that she would be able to defend herself if she was attacked. She worked hard and got one belt after another. Later, when she was attacked, she slugged the man with her purse!

If I get one thing I can use—make a part of my life—in a weekend, it has been a good weekend for me. If I remember the whole thing and don't *use* any of it, then all I can do is talk about it. Lost weekend.

After this weekend, I sometimes reminded myself to have soft eyeballs. Now I am reminded quite often—the reminder seemingly not my own doing—to let my eyeballs be soft. They become soft when I notice them. The whole thing does itself.

During one session I thought "This is a great place to come to learn how to lead a group." It can't be copied or followed. If I make myself do what Rinpoche did, then I am copying and by definition a copy cannot be original. Besides, how can I copy him when he keeps doing something else? What I can do is break with the thoughts that keep me from being my own original.

A questioner asked a very long and involved question that I could not follow. If the question had been asked of me, I probably would have said that I did not understand, asked for clarification, and so on. There's a good chance that I would also be critical of myself for not understanding the question. When the question was asked of Rinpoche, he did not respond immediately. His torso and head moved away from the questioner. He rubbed his fingers vigorously through his short hair, then smoothed it back with his palm. I don't know if this was a simple human gesture or if he was stirring up the chakras or both. Then he looked at the questioner and said "Too much." The essence. He said it as a statement of fact, with the neutrality and lack of judgment that is its own form of expression.

Glenn told me that when he was in a six-week seminar with Rinpoche, he became very distressed with his personal life and poured this out to Rinpoche. At the end Rinpoche said, with the same neutrality, simple observation, "You have emotionals." Glenn saw the whole thing then and burst out laughing. When I see my own "emotionals," that's so clearly what they are—my fears, prejudices, conditioning, and lord knows what else—embroidering all around the facts, like writing a novel about myself and suffering for the person I'm writing about. Carl Rogers wrote years ago "The facts are always friendly." Indeed they are, when I don't dress them up with costumes and invent a plot and Problems that keep the whole thing going.

I fell asleep during a lecture. Rinpoche may have said things while I wasn't there that were as important as his few words often were to me—like "Grasping makes problems." Indeed, I could write a long and comprehensive explanation of why I went to sleep. The fact is, I was sleepy.

Happiness is the feeling that nothing is required of me—and that I require nothing of myself. That doesn't mean that I don't *do* anything.

Great discovery!
 Wonder if it will be true tomorrow?

I have no regrets for my life. Certainly I would do many things different if I were to do them now, but I couldn't *then* because I didn't know they were mistakes or I wouldn't have made them. So everything was all right because of what I learned through doing things wrong as well as right.

It doesn't matter which way you choose as long as you remember how to swim. You may want to change course.

I thought that I understood yin and yang: The one was the gentle side of a person, the other the strong side. But the acupuncturist uses them differently. I asked him about that today when he said that mangoes were yin. I said they had seemed pretty yang to me, particularly when they blistered my lips and fingers. He said "Oh yes, but it is in what they produce in a person afterward that is gentle." Sort of like Zap! I clobber you and afterwards you are gentle.

That's as far as he went. I'm sure he would have corrected my last statement if we had gone farther. In any case, it's just a concept—a tool. What else are words but tools? Yin/yang expresses another duality. The circle that encloses both represents the whole. And that's another concept.

There's nothing wrong with concepts if we don't confuse them with reality. I laugh, and with both hands play an imaginary viola. As there is no instrument, I don't have to shift it when I switch hands and play it from the other side. What a jest!

When my husband and I first met it seemed very unlikely we would be together for long. That was the best time of our lives together. We had no future and no past. No yesterday and no tomorrow. We enjoyed each moment as though that was all there was. Then the snake of time—which has no existence except as a manmade invention for convenience—slithered into the Garden of Eden.

The way that I experienced things that happened in my life after the age of forty was that every time I got up on my knees, I was pushed flat on my face. The way that others saw the same events was "Every time you fall down, you land on your feet."

What we both would agree on was that my life seemed to fall apart disastrously and somehow it got together again. I'm still here.

Each time, I was—after the falling apart and the getting together again—so far ahead in my knowing about life and myself that it seemed I had learned a lesson, one specifically designed for me.

Obviously I needed it.

It now seems to me that I engineered the whole thing myself.

It can be construed in many ways. Which one is real?

None, I suspect.

Albert Einstein said that the world that we have made as a result of the levels of thinking that we've done this far creates problems that we cannot solve at the same level as the level at which we created them. I'm sure that I don't know what Einstein meant by that statement and equally sure that I have benefitted by coming across it. I have been looking for a level different from the one that I created my problems at, in order to solve them.

Of course! The third eye—which is the *whole* mind—looks over the *whole* scene without perturbation *or* excitation.

I'm not afraid now that something will be lost without them. We don't have a word for what comes in their place. That doesn't make it non-existent.

When I was sick, my dis-ease was non-existent because medically there wasn't a name for it. It was there just the same.

So is the lilting of my knowing in the second paragraph.

I could have got this answer two years ago or five years ago or ten or twenty if I were not so forgetful. Doesn't matter. Nothing matters when I know it *now*. *Now* the whole world is laughing with me and the sound vibrates throughout my body. I open the window and shout "I'm here!" and it doesn't matter that nobody hears me. I am my own doing and laughter ripples through my chest.

The colors of the world ripple outside my window with names like columbine pink yellow cedar brown green lily of the valley grass hawthorne . . .

When I remember the names again I'm not here any more. The rippling has left.

The perennial Now is hardly ever perceived without the distortions and contaminations introduced into it by the mind from past experience and future expectations. Throughout this book we have seen how assumptions, beliefs, premises, superstitions, hopes and the like may become more real than reality, creating that web of delusions called *maya* in Indian philosophy. Thus, to empcy himself, to free himself from the involvement with past and future, is the goal of the mystic.

Paul Watzlawick

good	*bad*
justify	*condemn*
praise	*blame*
love?	*hate*
not this	*not that*

what else is there?

Carl Rogers   *Fritz Perls*

Barry

When I was acting as therapist, in the beginning when I got stuck and didn't know what to do, I thought in panic "What would Carl do?" I didn't know. Then I'd switch to "What would Fritz do?" Same no answer. That left me with nothing to think—or follow—and out of *myself* the answer would come and I did it.

So that's what all this "not this/not that" is about!

What else is there?
ME
me
not me
NOT ME
the universe

The future would mean that there is something that is *going to happen,* a "fate." The minute you "see" a future you would necessarily change it by reacting, so it wouldn't be the same future.

Can you work towards the future? It seems to me false to channel your life. You in reality work in any direction from 0 degrees, which is where you are now.

But "now" doesn't exist. You are walking backward into a hurricane and can only tell which way to go by the debris that flies past you. Or you are blown about in this hurricane, judging only the past whether you look into the wind or with it. If you "see it coming" you have already reduced it to a judgment of the past—since all judgments are necessarily of *past* experience.

Best not to worry about direction at all. Just be. Direction is already there.

Jim Fiddes

If you look at a person who is giving a gift to someone else, it is quite clear who is the giver and who is the receiver and our largely objective language attached the appropriate words: Thank you. You're welcome. Each person knows the correct response according to who is which at the time.

To the Hawaiians there was no difference—giver and receiver were the same, so the correct word to say was the same for both: *Mahalo*. Something going on between us. You are happy with receiving and I am happy with your receiving which feels like a gift to me.

Mahalo.

Mahalo.

Equal. No tilted words of giver and receiver, benefactor and beneficiary, one looking down on and the other looking up to.

If you give me an elaborate present, we are even. When I give you a token, we are even. Each time clears itself.

Mahalo—Mahalo.

No tilt.

Equal.

We've got to take a big leap to get out of the mess we're in. *I've* got to take a big leap. As I know this, a lot of other people know it too. Some have undoubtedly already leaped. I would like to know who they are and what their leap was to make it easier for me to leap. But then it wouldn't be my own leap.

> Many paths will take you
> halfway up the mountain.
> Only your path will
> take you to the top.
>
> *Clint Weyand*

My path—the path of any me—is *no* path. Going a way once does not make a path.

No one else can find it. I can't even find it myself and do it over. Fortunately that makes it impossible to tell you how you should go. I don't know.

I am no longer timid about stating what I see and what I am doing.

I'm seeing what I can learn about regeneration. I know that it's possible for this eighty-two-year-old body to regenerate itself. To some extent, it does that all the time. Otherwise I wouldn't be here. I want to find out how to let it do more so. I don't know if I shall find the clue that will make it possible for me, but already I have run into some surprising developments that have no place in *this* book.

Procrastination.

Until yesterday I would have said that I don't have any.

I called a friend to help me through the final stages of this book. By talking to him, he gets something clear in me and I move. I don't know how he does this. I think he doesn't know either. But at the end of a fairly brief conversation I was able to start work again without tying myself in knots.

This time, he listened to my plight and said that he envied me, that he is a procrastinator while I stay with things and get them done.

I went back to work on the business of making a book—the tedious part—the mechanical part—of arranging the pages and then making the arrangements consistent throughout three copies and so on. I can give all the *becauses* that make this difficult just now. A big one is that I want to get on with regeneration.

As I went on working, I noticed how and what I put off "in order to get the job done." When I got hungry, I put off eating. When I needed to go to the bathroom, I put it off. My eyes were tired and needed a rest and exercise—movement instead of the staring that I get into. I put that off too. My body needed to stretch and I held it tightly in a cramped position, not getting up to walk around.

Putting off, putting off, putting off . . .

Suddenly I realized what I was doing! I went to the telephone and called my friend. "I'm a procrastinator too!" I told him. "It's the other side of the coin!"

"I get *approved* for *my* procrastination because the society we live in approves of it. I'm sure you get criticized for doing the same thing that I do," I told him. "In a society with different values you would find approval and I would be damned."

I thought of my Chilean friends who did not often let work interfere with living.

This morning I have so little time it scares me. "I'll never get anything done." Yet the yesterday which was Sunday I lazed through most of the day—a little annoyed that I couldn't do anything on the book—made soup for lunch and before I could eat it was—I was about to say invited but I think I invited myself—to go to the lake, and rice cakes and a banana went with me.

It was a beautiful hour with sunshine on one side of the lake and pine trees on the other already in shade. I enjoyed it—and enjoyed walking for twenty minutes, later for another five. It feels good to walk on uneven ground. There was no obligation to walk, as there has been: I must walk because walking is good for me and on those terms it isn't. I made that mistake so often the past winter and spring.

I came home and fixed supper and did dishes and lo! a space appeared in this house which hadn't been there before and I set out the manuscript in three piles with room to turn the pages. I went through the whole thing before eleven o'clock by *stopping* when I needed to rest, taking myself *away* from the work, reading a mystery story . . .

This morning I feel easy and it's ten o'clock and I am eating breakfast and writing this to be typed later and thinking "I'll *never* get the book done this way" and ignoring my thinking and going ahead with what I'm doing and the way I'm doing it and I just noticed that my eyes feel better and my vision is improved—even the eye which has to look around a cataract. My fingers are less clumsy.

And all this came about when Paul said "I'm a procrastinator" and the sky split open and let me see my own procrastination.

This book does and doesn't end. In one sense it does: There are no more pages with words on them. In another sense, no book ever ends. It goes on in the minds of the readers, mingles with the thoughts of others, changes form—until the origin of ideas contained in it has got lost.

The first end is arbitrary though this is not usually stated. I am ending this book because I want to focus on learning a new (to me) way of behaving with regard to my body. It will take most of my time/energy for a month assimilating the new instructions before I can fully use them. Then, when they have become a part of me, there will be at least six months of observation of myself in a new mode to see what's happening. Whether I shall learn what I think I may or something else entirely remains to be seen. The only impossible is nothing.

I don't have any sparkling words to close with

so

    I

        just

            dribble

                off

This morning I woke up with a feeling of completion of far more than this book.

When I was a child, I got into terrible trouble with the notion that other people seemed to have that the way to live is doing what *other* people want me to do. This made no sense to me. I would see the world as a globe with people sticking out all over it and everyone was bowing to everyone else and doing what *they* wanted him to do. *Nobody* was doing what *he* wanted to. All the circuits in my brain would short out. Fizzzzcracklespit and blackness shot with searing light. My behavior would get worse and worse and the harder I tried to stop the bad behavior the worse it got. I was in despair and longed for mother to spank me. I hated the spanking but longed for the peace that followed. When mother at last spanked me, I yelled like hell until I was exhausted, then gently cried my way back into sunshine again.

So now, this search has ended. Throughout my life, it has gone on like an undercurrent that surfaces and becomes current then goes under again. Now I feel at rest. No longer is it a problem.

Rejecting both selfishness and unselfishness, I get beyond. I sigh with relief—or is it satisfaction? Now, the foreground of my interest slips into the background and a new foreground—which had been lurking in the wings—takes over. How orderly is life! Nothing is wasted. I see it now.

Yesterday when I went for a walk, my legs wanted to run. They haven't felt like running for years and years. I think 1951 was the last year that I ran for pleasure, for the happiness of good feeling. Regeneration? I am eager to find out.

I am gurgling like a baby or a brook.

Is there a difference?

April 1983

This book has been finished for six months. Just now I am going over it for things to say more clearly than I did, and so on. Yesterday Cherry drove me to the airport to meet a plane. The plane was several hours late. We went to a bookstore. Then she asked me if I would rather have something to drink or go to another bookstore. I voted for another bookstore, not making sense to me at the time because my eyes were tired, I didn't want to look at books, I wasn't looking for a particular book.

At the second bookstore, I saw Krishnamurti's *Flight of the Eagle,* which I had read in 1971. I bought it.

Yesterday after meeting the plane was guest-busy and this morning also. When the flurry of departure was over I picked up the book and by chance opened it to page 31, where I found the following, which was exactly what I needed to set things straight in the manuscript, as you will see. It's like finding a jewel, more precious and more light-giving than a diamond. I expand. I breathe more freely.

"Please do not accept or deny what the speaker is saying, just examine it. The speaker—let us again be definite about that matter—has no value whatsoever. It's like a telephone, you do not obey what the telephone says. The telephone has no authority, but you listen to it. Do not accept or deny, but observe and listen, not only to what is being said but also to your reactions, to your distortions, as you are listening; see your prejudices, your opinions, your images, your experiences, see how they are going to prevent you from listening."

I have an image of Krishnamurti galloping across the sky. That's *my* image. It says something to me. I kiss it goodbye. I've got the message.

There are two ways of exercising your mind. The other way is to chew over everything you read.

This leaves out the best of me—which isn't me.

Burst out laughing.

No *I!*

Since mind-as-such
pure from the beginning
and with no root to hold to
something other than itself—
has nothing to do with
an agent or something
to be done, one's mind
may well be happy.

Since intrinsic awareness
with no objective reference whatsoever,
has no intention as to this or that,
one may well be full of love toward all.

Since vision and attention to the visitor
are not disrupted nor falling into contraries,
having nothing to do with
acceptance or fear, high or low,
one may well be joyous.

Since enactment and goal,
having nothing to do with
acceptance and rejection, expectation
and anxiety, are not seen as something
to be obtained or missed,
one may well feel an inner warmth.

Since everything is but an apparition,
perfect in being what it is,
having nothing to do with good or bad,
acceptance or rejection,
one may well burst out in laughter.

                                        Long-chen-pa

Richard P. Feynman asked to be identified by name only and this is so much in accord with the spirit of this book that I went through the manuscript and removed other identification throughout.

As usual, some things just don't fit, and I have added this section to accommodate them.

Focusing, by Eugene T. Gendlin, University of Chicago, is both the title of a book (Bantam) and the name of a method of getting beyond the dualities that plague all of us (with the possible exception of Krishnamurti). Gendlin's "felt meaning" is equated with David Bohm's "implicate order," which makes Bohm a lot clearer to me.

Gendlin also has a manuscript that will probably be in print by the time this is. (In the meantime it can be obtained by writing him direct.) He says the experts can't decide, so *Let Your Body Interpret Your Dreams*. Why not? It's your body that dreams them.

The Krishnamurti quotations are from *Flight of the Eagle* (Harper & Row).

The quotations from Paul Watzlawick are all from his book *How Real Is Real*—"confusion, disinformation, communication—an anecdotal introduction to communications theory" (Vintage Books). I read the chapters from *The Trials of Translation* to *Time Travel* with delight, with no thought of where they were leading—no anticipation that they would culminate in *The Perennial Now*. Then they all fell into place.

Of course I might have read the table of contents but I usually don't.